INCULTURATION

Working Papers on Living Faith and Cultures

edited by

Arij A. Roest Crollius, S.J.

VIII

This issue has been published in collaboration with the Centre for Coordination of Research of the International Federation of Catholic Universities (F.I.U.C.) and with the help of Konrad Adenauer Foundation.

CENTRE "CULTURES AND RELIGIONS" - PONTIFICAL GREGORIAN UNIVERSITY

Arij A. Roest Crollius – Paul Surlis
Thomas Langan – Rodger Van Allen

CREATIVE INCULTURATION AND THE UNITY OF FAITH

ROME 1986

Paul Surlis, Associate Professor of Moral Theology and Social Ethics at St. John's University, New York, since 1975. Contributed to "Morals, Law and Authority". Edited "Faith: Its Nature and Meaning". Recent articles include "Politicization of Youth"; "The New Name for Nuclear Weapons is sin"; "Religion and Society". Awarded Von Humboldt Foundation Fellowship and studied at University of Munster 1970-71. Was "Peritus" at concluding session of Second Vatican Council, 1965 with Bishop T.J. Drury of Corpus Christi, Texas.

Thomas Langan is Professor of Philosophy, University of Toronto, Canada, former president, American Catholic Philosophical Association, and The Metaphysical Society of America, and a member of the editorial board of "Communio", North America. He is author or co-author of six books in the area of modern and recent philosophy, and of fifty articles. He has been active in development work in Columbia and Niger.

☆

Rodger Van Allen is Professor of Religious Studies at Villanova University, Villanova Pennsylvania, U.S.A. He wrote "The Commonwealth and American Catholicism, and edited "American Religious Values and the Future of America". He was founding Co-Editor of "Horizons", and served as President of the College of Theology Society 1982-1984.

TABLE OF CONTENTS

PRESENTATION

This issue of INCULTURATION entitled "Creative Inculturation and the Unity of Faith" presents three studies which were read
and discussed during the Jerusalem seminar of FIUC in 1985.

The first study by Paul Surlis is "The Relation Between Social
Justice and Inculturation in the Papal Magisterium"; the second one
"Accomodating Culture Without Dissolving the Unity of the Faith"
was presented by Thomas Langan; the third contribution on
"Catholicism in the United States: Some Elements of Creative
inculturation" was given by Rodger Van Allen.

By way of introduction, a brief study by the Editor has been
added which is an effort to formulate the problem of doctrinal unity
within a pluricultural church.

It is evident that these working papers do not necessarily
represent a common opinion of all the participants in the Jerusalem
seminar and neither of the editors of INCULTURATION.

At the request of several of our readers we publish here also the
list of the participants of the 1985 seminar of FIUC and also that of
the participants of the Yogyakarta seminar of 1983.

Arij A. Roest Crollius, S.J.

Symposium on:

INCULTURATION: THE CHRISTIAN EXPERIENCE
AMIDST CHANGING CULTURES

(Tantur, September 22-26, 1985)

LIST OF PARTICIPANTS

Arij A. ROEST CROLLIUS S.J.	Project Leader
	Pontificia Università Gregoriana, Roma
Maria de la Cruz AYMES, S.H.	San Francisco, Ca., USA
Kees BERTENS, M.S.C.	Atma Jaya Catholic University
	Jakarta, Indonesia
William E. BIERNATZKI, S.J.	Sogang University
	Seoul, Korea
Francis J. BUCKLEY, S.J.	University of San Francisco, Ca.. USA
Dinh-duc DAO	Università Urbaniana, Roma (Vietnam)
George A. DE NAPOLI, S.J.	Pontificia Università Gregoriana, Roma
Marcel DUMAIS, O.M.I.	Université Saint-Paul
	Ottawa, Canada
Rosemary GOLDIE	Pontifical Council for Laity, Roma
	(Australia)
Ignatius HIRUDAYAM, S.J.	Madras, India
Adriano IRALA BURGOS	Universidad Católica «Nuestra Señora
	de Asunción», Asunción, Paraguay
Maria Elena Chiong-JAVIER	De la Salle University Manila, Philippines
Peter KNECHT, S.V.D.	Nanzan University
	Nagoya, Japan
Thomas LANGAN	St. Michael's College
	Toronto, Canada
Bernardino LEERS, O.F.M.	Minas Gerais, Brazil
Eugenio MAURER AVALOS, S.J.	Centro de Estudio Educativos, A.C.
	México, D.F., Mexico
Charles NYAMITY	CHIEA, Nairobi, Kenya
Janusz PASIERB	Akademia Teologii Katolickiej
	Warzawa, Poland
Paul SURLIS	St. John's University Jamaica, N.Y.,
	USA
Andrzej SWIĘCICKI	Warzawa, Poland
Rodger VAN ALLEN	Villanova University, Pa., USA
A.M. VARAPRASADAM, S.J.	St. Joseph's College
	Tiruchirapalli, India
Judy VAN ALLEN	Academic Secretary, Villanova, Pa., USA
Marina PAGLINO	Executive Secretary, Roma

Seminar on:

CHRIST AND CULTURES

(Yogyakarta, June 23 - July 2, 1983)

LIST OF PARTICIPANTS

J. B. Banawiratma, S.J.	Vedabhakti Faculty of Theology, Yogyakarta
Karl J. Becker, S.J.	Gregorian University, Rome
Augustinus Gianto, S.J.	Cambridge, Mass., USA
John F. Gorski, M.M.	La Paz, Bolivia
R. Hardawiryana, S.J.	Vedabhakti Faculty of Theology, Yogyakarta
T. Jacobs, S.J.	Vedabhakti Faculty of Theology, Yogyakarta
Martin Mudendeli, S.J.	Kinshasa, Zaïre
Joseph Prasad Pinto, OFM Cap.	Naini Tal, India
Arij A. Roest Crollius, S.J.	Gregorian University, Rome
Pedro C. Sevilla	Ateneo de Manila University, Manila
Joseph Shih, S.J.	Gregorian University, Rome
Köshi Usami, S.J.	Sophia University, Tokyo
Adam Wolanin, S.J.	Gregorian University, Rome

Arij A. Roest Crollius, S.J.

INCULTURATION FROM BABEL TO PENTECOST

(An Introduction)

Unity of Doctrine – Plurality of Expressions

One of the reasons for the Extraordinary Assembly of the Bishop's Synod in 1985 was the theological interpretation of the doctrine of Vatican II in view of a deeper reception of the Council. This work of theological interpretation has highlighted the importance of inculturation. The Final Report of the Synod speaks of "the theological principle for the problem of inculturation." This theological principle becomes manifest in the "paschal perspective" which brings about "a missionary openness for the integral salvation of the world." Inculturation, according to the Synod, "is different from a simple external adaptation, because it means the intimate transformation of the authentic cultural values through their integration in Christianity and through the taking root of Christianity in various human cultures." These words show clearly that inculturation is not "simple," but is a "two-way process": from cultures to Christianity and from Christianity to cultures. Inculturation is, at the same time, a process of integration and of taking root. And since cultures are many, and Christian doctrine is one, the problem is given of the one and the multiple.

The Theological Principle of Inculturation

The question with which we are concerned in these pages can be expressed as follows: "To what point can inculturation of the doctrine of the faith go?" And the answer is very simple, so long as one clearly understands the meaning of "inculturation": "Inculturation of the doctrine of the faith is a never-ending task and can know no other limits than those of the breadth of all humanity, which is to be gathered into the unity of the one people of God."

In order to understand the meaning of this statement, one must bear in mind the theological principle stated in the text issued by the

3

Synod: inculturation is not some superficial adaptation, but is, rather, a "two-way" process through which Christianity takes root within cultures and cultural values are integrated into Christianity. The "hinge point" between these two dynamics is the interior transformation and the regeneration of cultural values. The two dynamics of taking root and integration are necessary to one another in the process of inculturation. Without the deep and never-ending taking root of Christianity within human cultures, inculturation would stay on the surface of the life of a people, which would result in that rift between gospel and culture that Paul VI referred to as the "drama of our time" (*Evangelii Nuntiandi* 20). Christian unity — or, better, the appearance of unity — would be a surface uniformity which did not touch the soul of the peoples. On the other hand, without the integration of cultural values into Christianity, the rooting of Christianity within cultures would be equivalent to a mere scattering. Limiting oneself to the details of individual cultures and forgetting the aim of communication through transformed and regenerated cultures would inevitably lead to divisions. We also note in passing that the one-sided emphasis on the mystery of the incarnation as "model" for the encounter between gospel and cultures can easily lead to a particularistic and particularizing conception of the process of inculturation. One must therefore bear in mind the whole mystery of Christ, and especially the paschal event, which is the wellspring of trasforming and life-giving energy for human situations and structures.

In other words, without the transformation of cultural values and their integration into the Christian and ecclesial communion, the rooting of Christianity within cultures would follow alone the lines of the dispersion of Babel. In the full sense, inculturation is going the way from Babel to Pentecost: not a return to the situation prior to Babel, when "the whole earth had one language and few words" (Gen. 11:1), but entering into a new communion which is actually brought about through the plurality of different expressions: "We hear them telling in our own tongues the mighty works of God" (Acts 2:11).

Inculturation is thus both rooting and integration, propagation and gathering in, sowing and harvesting. And union is brought to these dual concepts by the slow process and patient work of transformation and regeneration of cultural values in contact with Christian faith and life.

4

In this way, the preceding statement (that is, that inculturation of the doctrine of the faith is a never-ending process) becomes clearer. The expression of the doctrine of the faith is always situated within a specific cultural context. The primordial and model fact is the actual event of revelation. The Second Vatican Council says: "Indeed the words of God, expressed in the words of men, are in every way like human language, just as the Word of the eternal Father, when he took on himself the flesh of human weakness, became like men" (*Dei Verbum* 13). Since then, certain expressions of the doctrine of the faith (symbols of the faith, dogms and definitions of Councils) have taken on a truly universal and trans-cultural meaning: the expression itself serves as a universal point of reference. Other expressions of doctrine do not in themselves have this type of trans-cultural meaning and function. Every expression of revealed truth — scripture, magisterium or theological elaboration — bears this resemblance to the way people speak.

Now, coming to resemble the way people speak also means entering the multiform world of human cultures and of the various languages in which these cultures are expressed. The fact which is observed in the text of sacred scripture and in the Pentecost event; is, in an analogous manner, still a feature of the tradition and exposition of the doctrine of the faith in the communion of the Apostolic Churches. The Council recognized that "In the study of revealed truth East and West have used different methods and approaches in understanding and confessing divine things. It is hardly surprising, then, if sometimes one tradition has come nearer to a full appreciation of some aspects of a mystery of revelation than the other, or has expressed them better. In such cases, these various theological formulations are often to be considered complementary rather than conflicting" (*Unitatis Redintegratio* 17). And this is not merely a statement about the past. The Council also encouraged theologians to proceed with proper freedom: "While preserving unity in essentials, let everyone in the Church, according to the office entrusted to him, preserve a proper freedom ... in the theological elaborations of revealed truth" (*Unitatis Redintegratio* 4). Such freedom is also recommended for pastoral reasons, in other words, in order for communication and celebration of the faith to be in greater harmony with the character of the various nations and better adapted to fostering the good of souls (cf. *Unitatis Redintegratio* 16).

In extremely clear and courageous terms, the Council applied these principles to the Churches in cultural areas which have only recently come in contact with Christianity: "... in each of the great socio-cultural regions, as they are called, theological investigation should be encouraged and the facts and words revealed by God, contained in sacred Scripture, and explained by the Fathers and Magisterium of the Church, submitted to a new examination in the light of the tradition of the universal Church" (*Ad Gentes* 22). This work of new examination (*novae investigationi subiiciantur*) has hardly begun and will occupy generations of theologians to come.

In this understanding the previously cited "theological principle of inculturation" will also be born in mind: that is, the "two-way" principle which means the taking root of Christianity within cultures and the integration of cultural values into Christianity through a process of transformation. As examples, various consequences of this principle can be noted. In the first place, when facts and words of revelation are expressed in a new language, they receive a new resonance within the framework of the literary tradition of a people. Even in simple translation, the principle of analogy must be born in mind — and this is even truer when producing new theological elaborations. Here we have one of the preconditions for communication in the multicultural and universal Church. In the second place, the plurality of theological elaborations needs specific instruments in order to ensure unity within the one Church. A permanent conference of theologians, biblical scholars, philosophers and men of letters, which would be truly pluri-cultural and pluri-disciplinary, could be a very effective instrument. In the third place, while in a number of sciences an ever greater uniformity can be observed on various levels (terminology, language, planning, etc.), theologians too should respond to the challenge to produce theological elaborations and expressions which are authentically universal. Although we are convinced that not only does legitimate pluriformity not constitute an obstacle to unity but is indeed its articulate manifestation, we are just as certain that this same unity requires its own universal expressions.

Cowardice and haste are bad counsellors in this vast work, in which patience and courage are needed. The aim is not a becoming fragmented in particularisms nor a being dissolved into a grey uniformity; it is, rather, that Catholic universality which accepts all the spiritual riches of the peoples, and purifies, consolidates and elevates them, leading them to unity (cf. *Lumen Gentium* 13).

Arij A. Roest Crollius, S.J.

Paul Surlis

THE RELATION BETWEEN SOCIAL JUSTICE AND INCULTURATION IN THE PAPAL MAGISTERIUM

Introduction

Study of papal social teaching shows that, since the Second Vatican Council, "culture", with its subsidiary "inculturation", has been added to such key-concepts as "peace", "social-justice", "social love" and "liberation" in the social encyclicals. "Culture" is a slippery term and its usage in the context of social teaching may represent only that one other topic is being added to those already listed. But "Culture" may also be an integrating concept, if not the integrating concept, or architectonic principle in papal teaching on the church's mission and social questions.

Before trying to decide which of the above best describes papal appeal to culture in social teaching let us first trace some of the factors which led to the emergence of culture as a subject of theological concern in Vatican II. One of these factors is the insistence by popes from Leo XIII on, that indigenous clergy should be trained and ordained for mission territories. This policy ensured the presence of indigenous bishops at Vatican II. They in turn, helped foster a theology of mission, culture and the local church which was given impetus in the subsequent social theology of Paul VI, Synods, Medellin and Puebla and now in the writings and discourses of John Paul II. Two questions will be addressed to Pope John Paul's teaching: Is recourse to culture an evasion of the tough social, political, economic and violence-related issues which threaten our world or is the focus on culture a necessary measure to ensure that these issues are addressed in all their complexity? The second question is: are papal and curial practice, especially when they are centralizing, bureaucratic and repressive, compatible with teaching which emphasizes true freedom, the full panoply of human rights and genuine pluralism? — all of which pertain to culture and inculturation as we propose to show.

Indigenous Priests

Since its inception in 1622 the Congregation for the Propagation of the Faith has had as its formal policy that many indigenous aspects of people's lives in foreign countries should not be arbitrarily changed by missionaries. In 1659, missionaries were told: "Do not regard it as your task and do not bring any pressure to bear upon the people to change their manners, customs and uses, unless they are evidently contrary to religion and sound morals." It was recognized that people "love and treasure... their own country and that which belongs to it; in consequence there is no stronger cause for alienation and hate than an attack on local customs, especially when these go back to venerable antiquity." That the situation was very accurately assessed is clear from the observation that alienation is increased "when an attempt is made to introduce the customs of another people in place of those which have been abolished." [1]

Assumptions of European superiority remained strong, however, and time and again the popes condemned attitudes that would regard local people as inferior or that judged local men to be unfit for priesthood. But, insist the popes did and the case for indigenous clergy is made repeatedly and strongly from the papacy of Leo XIII on. Several reasons for indigenous clergy were given: their superior knowledge of local languages and customs and hence their ability to preach the Gospel more effectively. Moreover, experience taught that in times of political upheaval, while foreign missionaries might be expelled, indigenous clergy would not and so it was expedient to have them to ensure stability. Still, the elite seminarians were sent to Rome for theological formation and frequently it was from these or from the canonists also trained in Rome that indigenous bishops were chosen.

Local customs may have been respected by missionaries at the Vatican's behest but local religions which were not regarded as instruments of salvation for their adherents were not. Leo XIII tended to equate culture with civilization and to see the Church as

---

[1] *Collectanea S. Congregationis De Propaganda Fide* (Rome 1907) Vol. 1, p. 42. Cited by Stephen Neill: *A History of Christian Missions* (Harmondsworth: Penguin Books, 1964) p. 179.

the most effective agent in the advancement of civilization. He credits the Church with having put an end to slavery "civilized the human race, freed it from degradation, and with all care trained it to a way of living such as befits the dignity and the hopes of man." (*INSCRUTABILI* §5)[2]. Leo defends the Church as an ally of progress and the friend of civil governments as thoroughly as its critics attacked the Church as obscurantist and reactionary.

Benedict XV (in *Maximum Illud* 1919) is concerned for approximately one billion non-believers who 'dwell in the shadow of death' ignorant of Christ and the 'divine blessings of redemption' brought by him. Preaching the Gospel to convert the pagans and save them from damnation was what was stressed as the purpose of missions. Gradually, as all know, the planting of the local church with its clergy and hierarchy was added, though perhaps in a subsidiary way, to the idea of preaching the Gospel.

The idea that the local church is a goal of missionary endeavor is strong in the encyclicals of Pius XII. In his writings also we are close to the modern idea of culture (which we shall see later). Still, Pius also speaks as if the Christian faith and superior Christian culture went hand in hand. He speaks of the church calling people to a "higher culture and a better way of life under the inspiration of the christian religion ..." [*Evangelii Praecones, (EP)* §56] In 1944 he wrote: "The herald of the gospel and the messenger of Christ is an apostle. His office does not demand that he transplant European civilization and culture, and no other to foreign soil, there to take root — and propagate itself. His task in dealing with these peoples, who sometimes boast of a very old and highly developed culture of their own, is to teach and form them so that they are ready to accept willingly and in a practical manner the principles of Christian life and morality; principles, I might add, that fit any culture, provided it be good and sound, and which give that culture greater force in safeguarding human dignity and in gaining human happiness."

We note here the assumption that 'principles of Christian life and morality' (cited again in *EP* §60) transcend cultural limitations. But are they also not to some extent expressed in the idiom of the

---

[2] Unless otherwise stated citations are from: *The Papal Encyclicals 1740-1981*, McGrath Publishing Co. Raleigh, VA. 5 volumes.

culture in which they are formulated and may they not also be influenced by ethnic and class biases? Let one example suffice: In 1866 a missionary bishop in Africa addressed questions to the Sacred Congregation of the Supreme Inquisition in Rome. One of his questions had to do with the practice of slavery and the answer was that "according to the approved theologians and commentators on the sacred cannons" it is "not contrary to natural and divine law for slaves, to be sold, bought, exchanged or given ... as long as they have moral certainty that those slaves have not been taken away from their lawful owner nor unjustly kidnapped into slavery." Eugene Hillman comments: "The inquisitors, with their astonishing respect for the sacredness of private property, carefully pointed out that it would be morally wrong for Christians to buy or accept slaves 'who had been stolen from their lawful owner' because 'it is wrong to buy property taken by theft'.

The same instruction, however, unambiguously condemned polygamy as being contrary to both "divine and natural law." [3] That wives and children dismissed from a polygamous household, when a chief converted to Christianity, might starve or be forced into prostitution in order to survive does not seem to have occurred to the inquisitors.

Still, despite inconsistencies and setbacks, progress was made in pre-conciliar mission theology. In 1936 Pius XI wrote: "It is necessary never to lose sight of the fact that the objective of the church is to evangelize not to civilize. If it civilizes it is for the sake of evangelization." [4] This emphasis on a spiritual mission with a supernatural goal represents an understanding of the church and its mission which was forged in response to Enlightenment attacks on revealed religion and on the role of the church. While, in one way or another, it is still with us in some ecclesiologies and in some people's consciousness it has today been supplanted in formal church teaching especially in the Post-Vatican II period. Pius XII, once

---

[3] Sacred Congregation of the Holy Office 'Instruction, June 20, 1866' cited by Eugene Hillman in "Towards the Catholicization of the Church" *The American Ecclesiastical Review* Vol. 168, No. 2. Feb. 1974, p. 128.

[4] *Semaines sociales de France* (Versailles, 1936) pp. 461-462; quoted in Walter M. Abbott, ed., *The Documents of Vatican II* (New York: America, 1966) p. 264, f. n. 192.

14

more, helped in the development toward a more socio-political understanding of the church's mission.

In 1956 he stressed the church's "strictly religious, supernatural goal" and he disclaimed any "mandate for the church in the cultural order." And yet in 1951 (in *Evangelii Praecones*) he was praising the work of medical missionaries (especially sisters) and he was encouraging lay involvement not only in the field of medicine but also in the area of "social reforms demanded by justice and charity." Pius XII was motivated in this social emphasis by his fear of the spread of communism in Europe and in mission territories but he was also sensitive to the "heart-felt cries that call for justice and a spirit of brotherly collaboration in a world made by a just God." And he stressed that social welfare programs alone, though praiseworthy, were not enough — there must be, he argues, *structural* change (to use today's expression) which is more a matter of justice than charity. "Charity indeed can remedy to a certain extent many unjust social condition. But that is not enough. For, in the first place, there must be justice which should prevail and be put into practice." (*EP* § 51).

Pius XII defends his plea for justice-related missionary work with reference to two recurring themes of his social teaching: the dignity of the human person and the right of all people to share the goods of the earth. He called for a new world economy and social order as pre-requisites for world peace (see "Christmas Message" December 1942) We see in his teaching clearly emerging the communal — global — purpose of the goods of the earth as one which takes precedence over the absolute right to private ownership: "The dignity of the human person then, speaking generally, requires as a natural foundation of life the right to the use of the goods of the earth. To this right corresponds the fundamental obligation to grant private ownership of property, if possible, to all". Pius XII called for legislation to achieve property transfer and by it, to rescue the worker ("who is or will be the father of a family"!) from an "economic dependence and servitude which is irreconcilable with his rights as a person." The context makes clear that Pius XII is arguing that agrarian reform is needed both to prevent the spread of communism and to maintain peace in mission lands. But — in view of the importance of this theme is the social teaching of John Paul II — it is important to note that Pius does not accept that answer

15

the lies in nationalization of property since that may be accompanied by manipulation of opinion and loss of freedom: "Whether this servitude arises from the exploitation of private capital or from state absolutism, the result is the same. Indeed, under the pressure of a state which dominates all and controls the whole field of public and private life, even going into the realm of personal opinions, projects and beliefs, the loss of liberty is so great that still more serious consequences can follow, as experience proves." (*EP*, 49-52) Pius XII is here touching on the theme of cultural exploitation for political and economic purposes but he does not consider how much this is also a feature of capitalism which may be more subtle in its approach but no less effective in being able to reach all areas of people's lives including the spiritual/cultural despite all talk of free individuals who are responsible for their own destiny.

Moreover, in his concern over the spread of Marxism to mission territories Pius XII showed little awareness of the historic relationship between colonial political exploitation and neo-colonial economic exploitation in third-world countries. In 1940 on the occasion of the eighth centenary of the independence of Portugal he wrote an encyclical in which he praised those countries "colonizing vigor and success in humanizing barbarous lands." (*Saeculo Exeunte Octavo*)

But still, his call for legislated land reform especially in mission territories was important. Coupled with his stress on the priority of the rights of all to use the goods of the earth over the rights of ownership of the few the pope's call for reform helped to distance official church teaching from the interests of powerful land owners who appealed to papal teaching on the absolute right to private property as a bulwark against the demands of the poor for justice.

John XXIII

Pope John XXIII's social teaching breaks new ground in several areas. Since what is relevant to our topic is found also in the Council and in the writings of Paul VI we shall offer the briefest outline here. John XXIII extended the range of the church's social agenda to include (albeit in a limited way), women, agricultural

16

workers and newer nations. He initiated a new openness to the world, a new spirit of dialogue and cooperation which extended to Marxists and all persons of good will. He placed the church firmly on the side of human rights in which he included as well as the civil liberties the socio-economic rights which, in some affluent countries are not regarded as on the same plane as the civil liberties or political rights as they are sometimes called.

Pope John's concern for peace, his denunciation of the arms race and of war as irrational in the atomic age, his vision of a world community founded on truth, justice, love, solidarity, and freedom are all relevant to assessing his impact on culture, in the broad sense.

His analysis of the breakdown in common or shared meaning between people, especially leaders of states, and the fear and destruction that may follow sets us on the way to seeing that the modern crisis is, properly understood, a cultural crisis and calls for a new analysis of religion and culture and their interrelationship. In a remarkable passage in *Pacem in Terris*, he shows how spiritual values underpin (or should since his description of society is an ideal one) all other social structures and arrangements; "Human society ... ought to be regarded above all as a spiritual reality; one in which men communicate knowledge to each other in the light of truth; in which they can enjoy their rights and fulfill their duties, and are inspired to strive for goods of the spirit. Society should enable men to share in and enjoy every legitimate expression of beauty. It should encourage them constantly to pass on to others all that is best in themselves, while they strive to make their own the spiritual achievements of others. These are the values which continually give life and basic orientation to cultural expressions, economic and social institutions, political movements and forms, laws and all other structures, by which society is outwardly established and constantly developed." (*Pacem in Terris* § 36)

Summary

On the eve of the Second Vatican Council, we perceive several shifts in progress on a complex set of themes which relate to our topic. The popes from Leo XIII up to and including John XXIII have encouraged the formation of indigenous clergy. They state the mission of the church as consisting both in preaching the Gospel and in building the local church over which the indigenous clergy would have full or equal control. The activity of mission is extended to lay persons especially so that they may engage in medical, education and social/welfare programs but also so that they may correct injustice by legal reforms and extension of the rights of property ownership.

The concept of culture, though still somewhat restricted to philosophy and aesthetics — high culture — is in transition to its modern understanding which is empirical and pluriform. The transcendence of the church's mission and message with reference to all cultures is affirmed. The reason for this transcendence is said to be in the spiritual and supernatural role of the church.

Clearly, unquestioned assumptions underly the foregoing Papal teaching which is deductive in its methodology and tends to be idealistic and abstract in its judgements. That Rome has a universal message for all missionary lands and that the message is disinterested and not conditioned by class, sexual or racial bias is implied in the texts.

Second Vatican Council

Several converging factors contributed to Vatican II's teaching on culture and inculturation. The latter word is not used but the idea of incarnating the gospel, with critical discernment in local cultures, is expressed. The purpose of this cultural enfleshment of the gospel is to enrich the local culture but also so that the 'world church' may be enriched by a variety of cultural richness.

The first of these converging factors was the *event* of the council itself which involved bishops meeting bishops from all over the world seeing daily liturgies, even in a limited variety of rites, and hearing the concerns of bishops from third-world countries expressed in St. Peter's. (The agenda of the council was mainly a first-world, liberal, agenda but that does not concern us immediately). The presence at the council of bishops, religious and priests who were indigenous members of "the missions" was the result of the policy of *Propaganda Fidei* and popes as we have seen.

18

In 1979 Karl Rahner argued that the presence of the indigenous bishops at Vatican II made that council the first council in which a 'world church' was represented and expressing itself and he proposed this as a fundamental principle for understanding Vatican II. By 'word church' Rahner means one that "begins to act through the reciprocal influence exercised by all its components."

The introduction of vernaculars into the liturgy is cited by Rahner as a signal of the coming into existence of this world church "whose individual churches exist with a certain independence in their respective cultural spheres, inculturated and no longer a European export." Rahner adds that a world church may experience new problems when "non-European local churches, for all their relationship to Rome, may no longer be ruled from Europe and its mentality."

What Rahner perceived in Vatican II as far as the transition of the church on to the world stage is concerned is something qualitatively new, analogous to, perhaps, one other such epochal transition namely, that from Jewish to Gentile Christianity effected largely by Paul in the apostolic age.[5]

Another converging factor, and one related to the preceding, is the development of the theology of the local church which is described in terms of its full ecclesial reality. The local church may no longer be regarded as an administrative sub-section of the 'real' church. The church, in Komonchak's words, is a concrete universal, whole in the whole and whole in each part.[6] But the local churches are constitutive of the universal church which lives *in* and *from* the particular churches. This means that the church is truly universal only insofar as it is localized or particularized and this not just spatially but with reference to customs, practices and life-style of the local people.

Vatican II on Culture

Related to the 'world-local' dynamic in the ecclesiology of Vatican II is the theology of culture which the council developed

---

[5] "Towards a Fundamental Theological Interpretation of Vatican II" *Theological Studies* Vol. 40. Dec. 1979, p. 716.

[6] "Ministry and the Local Church," Joseph Komonchak *Proceedings of the Catholic Theological Society of America 36th Annual Convention*, N.Y. 1982, pp. 56-82.

and which is found principally in *Gaudium et Spes*. Preparatory work on this schema was done by theologians and sociologists of religion and in the section on culture account was taken of the work of cultural anthropologists and ethnologists. The council offers several complementary descriptions rather than one definition of culture. The descriptions to justice to the classical and the modern empirical views of culture without becoming vague or nebulous as can be seen in this rather lengthy excerpt: "The word 'culture' in the general sense refers to all those things which go to the refining and developing of man's diverse mental and physical endowments. He strives to subdue the earth by his knowledge and his labor; he humanizes social life both in the family and in the whole civic community through the improvement of customs and institutions; he expresses through his works the great spiritual experiences and aspirations of men throughout the ages; he communicates and preserves them to be an inspiration for the progress of many, even of all mankind.

"Hence it follows that culture necessarily has historical and social overtones, and the word "culture" often carries with it sociological connotations; in this sense one can speak about a plurality of cultures. For different styles of living and different scales of values originate in different ways of using things, of working and self-expression, of practicing religion and of behavior, of establishing laws and judicial institutions, of developing science and the arts and of cultivating beauty. Thus the heritage of its institutions forms the patrimony proper to each human community; thus, too, is created a self-defined, historical milieu which envelops the men of every nation and age, and from which they draw the values needed to foster humanity and civilization." (*Gaudium et Spes* § 53-62)

Several points are high-lighted by the council: True and full humanity is achievable only through culture. All persons have a right to basic cultural benefits. Culture exists to serve integral personal and communal development — as well as that of the whole of society. Special attention should be paid to the cultural needs of the poor, women, laborers and minorities.

'Many links' are affirmed between the 'message of salvation and culture'. Revelation and church mission have utilized the cultures of the people they addressed. But the church has a universal

20

mission and is not bound exclusively and indissolubly to any race or nation, nor to any particular way of life or any customary pattern of living, ancient or living. Faithful to her other traditions and at the same time conscious of her universal mission, she can enter into communion with various cultural modes, to her own enrichment and theirs too. The gospel is not simply harmonized with culture which, as a product of fallen human beings, stands in need of purification and elevation. The Gospel acts as a leaven also in promoting civil culture.

The council stresses the autonomy of culture and the right that all persons, including members of the church, have to pursue truth in freedom and be correctly informed about public events. We are warned that culture should not be manipulated by public authorities for political and economic reasons.

The conciliar teaching on culture is positive and optimistic for the most part. It is also innocent of the histories of deliberate cultural destruction by colonizers (as e.g. Rome and England, in different ways, undermined Celtic Christianity in Ireland). It also fails to reflect the exclusion of women, native peoples and the poor from education, politics, and the arts through most of recorded history.

Critique

What are we to make of this conciliar teaching? One commentary on this section of *Gaudium et Spes* (in what amounts to an indictment of previous papal teaching) speaks of the difficulty of "relating this chapter on culture to papal documents anterior to it: For the first time, it seems, the church has been led to envisage social and cultural life as a whole, at the central meeting point of all its problems, economic, political, domestic, philosophical, religious, etc."[7] This 'cultural turn' has profound implications and part of what it means, I believe, is that the focus on culture in Vatican II is not one other new topic added to church teaching. Rather the

---

[7] *Constitution Pastorale "Gaudium et Spes"* par. "l'Action populaire" p. 214, n. 101 cited in *Commentary on the Documents of Vatican II*, H. Vorgrimler (ed.) Herder and Herder, N.Y. 1969, Vol. 5, p. 259.

manner in which culture is being spoken of forces us to recognize that *all* church teaching is social teaching. Exclusive attention to a limited number of papal encyclicals and treatment of them as if they alone contained the church's entire social teaching is false and misleading.

Papal teaching on sexuality, marriage, birth-control, divorce, abortion is social teaching since these realities all have social as well as personal dimensions. As teaching profoundly touching the lives of women papal thought on marriage and sexuality, especially must be seen as inescapably having political, economic and social dimensions even when this is not formally adverted to. Likewise, we may add, theology manuals and text books whether used in university or seminary courses are texts with unavoidable social dimensions and implications. However, up until recently social teaching was set off by itself. Systematic and moral theology, for example, were the major theological disciplines but were not regarded as social. Thus a false dichotomy was set up: on the one hand there was "theology" on the other hand there was "social teaching." Theology was regarded as being neutral where race, class, sexuality and politics were concerned — which of course it was not. The neutrality was only apparent; such theology invariably buttresses the *status quo* and affirms existing injustices by not addressing or questioning them. Anyone who doubts the truth of these assertions should reflect on the fact that most writing on Catholic Social Teaching omits any reference to the Holocaust. Most collections of papal social encyclicals for example do not even include Pius XI's encyclical *Mit brennender Sorge* (1937) written in condemnation of National Socialism in Germany. Also, the compliance with, not to say enthusiasm of some catholics for the genocidal policies of the Nazi party in Germany — and their enthusiasm for the not anti-semitic, but otherwise totalitarian regimes of Mussolini and Franco are not considered indictments of Catholic Social Teaching and morality. The "obedience to authority", civil and ecclesiastical, which has been granted *a priori* status of legitimacy and hammered into catholic consciousness, especially by the Vatican, has exacted a terrible price. There is the further consideration that thinking which is wrong about woman and her status and role in religion and society is formally wrong about 'half the human race' and in consequence, cannot be said to

22

have a global or comprehensive view of the *humanum* a claim made by Pope Paul VI and repeated by John Paul II on several occasions. Another reason for the relative lack of impact of papal and episcopal social proclamations lies in their isolation from mainstream theology the assimilation of which absorbs most of the energy of teachers, catechists and preachers even still. The theologies of liberation, overcome this false dichotomy but some of the suspicion and hostility with which they are greeted is directly related to the above problematic. All theology and religious practice should be liberationist if it is not it is oppressive whether selfconsciously or not is another matter.

What implications this has for social morality is slowly being worked out in the post-Vatican II documents on social justice and in the verbal teaching of Pope John Paul II on the evangelization of culture. Before we consider this further let us turn to the social teaching of Paul VI.

Paul VI

The internationalization of the church's view of the social question that was beginning to be evident in the social encyclicals of Pius XII and John XXIII was dramatically advanced in 1967 by Paul VI when he said "Today the principal fact that we must all recognize is that the social question has become world-wide." (*Populorum Progressio* §3) And he heard the hungry and exploited people of the world, particularly of the southern hemisphere, utter a cry of anguish to which he urged people to respond. The pope's personal visits to and contacts with the poor in Latin America, Africa and India had moved him deeply.

In analyzing the causes of global poverty Paul VI focussed first on the evils of colonialism which left behind dependence on one-crop economies that made the nations concerned vulnerable when prices for their export fell. Paul tries to be even-handed in his assessment of the effects of colonialism as he does in his assessment of the work of European missionaries overseas. He does focus on the collision between industrial civilization and traditional civilizations which sometimes disintegrate under the impact and deprive communities of needed support — structures in their lives.

"... The conflict of the generations is made more serious by a tragic dilemma: whether to retain ancestral institutions and convictions and renounce progress, or to admit techniques and civilizations from outside and reject, along with the traditions of the past, all their human richness. In effect, the moral, spiritual and religious supports of the past — too often give way without securing in return any guarantee of a place in the new world. (*PP* § 10)

Paul VI ignores the fact that many traditional languages, religions and cultural institutions were destroyed in the colonial period but he does place contemporary cultural issues in an economic and global context. "However, local and individual undertakings are no longer enough. The present situation of the world demands concerted action based on a clear vision of all economic, social, cultural and spiritual aspects" and he says, quoting Lebret "We do not believe in separating the economic from the human, nor development from the civilizations in which it exists." Paul highlights his approach as based on the concrete person in global context: "What we hold important is man, each man, and each group of men, and we even include the whole of humanity." (*PP* § 113-14)

At times Paul VI seems unaware of the constraints placed by unjust structures on the freedom of persons especially women and people of color and he speaks as if integral human development were simply a matter of the good will and efforts of each person. This in itself, is an interesting example of the pervasive influence of the capitalist myth of free individuals in a free market competing on equal terms where failure is to be attributed solely to personal lack of resolve. Paul VI saw that that was a myth in the time of Leo XIII with reference to workers and in his own day, as applied to nations, but he still writes in *Populorum Progressio* without adverting to the need for careful nuancing when personal freedom is being discussed. (*PP* § 15)

In the overall, however, Paul VI in *Populorum Progressio* shows awareness of the need both for moral conversion and for structural economic change at the international level. And while he advocated the virtues of solidarity with the oppressed and the need for education we cannot say that he sees in cultural analysis the integrating social role of which we have spoken. Indeed by culture he often appears to mean higher culture, artistic, intellectual and religious.

24

Paul VI's next major statement on social questions *Octogesima Adveniens* is unintelligible unless it is seen as a response to the Medellin declarations of 1968 so we turn briefly to these.

Medellin

The second general conference of Latin American Bishops was called to discuss the application of the Second Vatican Council's teaching to Latin America but soon the whole church was — and still is — being challenged by what emerged from Medellin.

Latin American theology of liberation preceded Medellin which injected its principal tenets into mainstream Catholic consciousness. Liberation theology grew out of the commitment of believing people to analyze, understand and transform their socio-economic situation in the light of in-depth understanding of the causes of their poverty and marginalization and in the light of the liberating traditions of scripture and faith.

Where previously popes (e.g. Pius XII) had said that the Gospel and the principles of morality can apply to all cultures, liberation theologians analyzed the structural causes of injustice, economic, political, social, sexual and religious and discerning the *demands* of the Gospel in such circumstances they are also recovering dimensions of the gospel and of faith that have been dormant or suppressed for centuries. Poverty, disease, illiteracy were not the will of God. They could far more correctly be described as consequences of foreign capitalist enterprises and local elites exploiting cheap resources and the cheap labor of the workers and peasants who were frequently kept unorganized, poor and ignorant by repressive governments who used appeals to the church's social teaching to defend the sacredness of private property and to outlaw rebellion which was condemned as unjust rebellion.

By 1968 many Latin Americans and other third-world thinkers had done a very thorough job of understanding their own socio-economic situation as one of dependency on the central or North Atlantic countries from which they were politically emancipated in the 19th century but to which they remained bound economically in the 20th century under a neo-colonial system that they did not hesitate to name and condemn.

25

It was also being clearly seen that the Christianity that came to Latin America in the 15th century was a Christendom Christianity. Monk and conquistador came together. This was not a meeting of cultures*; it was the invasion, suppression and despoliation of one culture by another that was militarily and technologically superior. Religion which came to Latin America under the protection of the crown and the sword served to legitimate a state of affairs that was frequently little short of servitude for the many for 500 years. At Medellin the voice of the non-person began to be heard and a church and religion that were political in their support of the status-quo began to change sides (not to take sides they had always done that) but to change from being on the side of the rich and powerful to being on the side of the powerless and exploited.

While undoubtedly there were many causes for the ferment in Latin America in the 60's one among them is worth mentioning since it is cultural in a somewhat narrow sense regarding the instrument used and is also in the wide genre of culture understood as the *complex whole* (Taylor), in its effects. This is the pedagogy of Paulo Freire which was instrumental in enabling people to understand their real socio-economic situation as one of exploitation and to discern the means of transforming their circumstances through action or praxis. Once critical consciousness of this sort is aroused who can again tame or confine it? This does not mean all revolutions must succeed but until major defeat is inflicted the struggle will go on. And inevitably in Latin America the base community churches come into existence frequently around relating faith and oppressive social conditions to put the matter baldly and broadly.

Part of Freire's pedagogy was enabling people to unmask falsehoods — especially those used to provide a smokescreen for exploitative behavior by elites who were benefitting from the status quo. The point here is that what appears to be "second nature" or even "natural" is frequently a characteristic or state of affairs engendered by an unjust economic or political system — the laziness and untrustworthiness of the Irish, the Blacks, the Indians etc. Critical consciousness searches deeply and fearlessly for all the

---

* This emphasis on cultural destruction as a consequence of colonialism was clearly expressed at Puebla 1969.

26

causes of oppression and it names them when they are uncovered. This makes it a very uncomfortable dialogue partner especially when the church and religion are named as being in collusion with the powerful. But — criticism does not mean rejection although, it is true, it should call for reformation.

What was Pauls VI's response?

Paul VI's Response

In 1971 he issued an apostolic letter entitled *Octogesima Adveniens* in which he reaffirmed the global nature of the problems but in which also he disclaimed having a universal solution:

"In the face of such widely varying situations it is difficult for us to utter a unified message and to put forward a solution which has universal validity. Such is not our ambition nor is it our mission." Instead, endorsing the method of liberation theology without naming it, the pope said: "It is up to the christian communities to analyze with objectivity the situation which is proper to their own country, to shed on it the light of the gospel's unalterable words and to draw principles of reflection, norms of judgment and directives for action from the social teaching of the church." Thus Paul VI had completed the second move of his social teaching — a return to the local. The problems are global in some respects but there is no universal answer. Local analysis, reflection and action — commitments are required and sanctioned, presumably, even if they involve commitments to socialism in one form or another. Now the local church is entrusted with the task of discovering its own most authentic form of witness to the values of the gospel which "is not out-of-date because it was proclaimed, written and lived in a different socio-cultural context." (*OA* §4)

A third shift effected by Paul VI in *Octogesima Adveniens* is the shift from economics to politics. In the fields of social and economic problems at the national and international levels, Paul argued, "the ultimate decision rests with political power" thereby recognizing that 'political' issues having to do with decision-making and structural change are power-related issues and touch on the structure and function of society and on the very nature, meaning and destiny of persons. But given the *control* which great financial

27

wealth is capable of exercising on the political process and on the persons who engage in politics it is questionable if one should push too hard the 'control' of economics by politics. The relationship seems to be rather more dialectical with economics often in the ascendancy although in a way that is masked or concealed. At all events, the pope circumscribes politics and places it in a wider cultural-religious matrix from which the deeper issues of life and its meaning are more approriately addressed and resolved. "It is not for the State or even for political parties, which would be closed unto themselves, to try to impose an ideology by means that would lead to a dictatorship over minds, the worst kind of all. It is for cultural and religious groupings, in the freedom of acceptance which they presume, to develop in the social body, disinterestedly and in their own ways, those ultimate convictions on the nature, origin and end of man and society." (*OA* §25)

Finally, we note that in *Octogesima Adveniens* Paul VI judged both technocratic capitalism and bureaucratic socialism as *systems* both of which failed to provid adequate models for people to live in just, peaceful societies and he called for utopian thinking to lend wings to the imagination and stimulate creative thinking about social issues, beyond ideologies. (§37)

Justice in the World

A synodal document, also issued in 1971 is of the highest importance in the church's social teaching. This declaration is to action on behalf of justice and peace in our time what Nicea or Chalcedon were to Christology in theirs. Working for social justice, in all its forms, is a "constitutive dimension of the preaching of the Gospel, or, in other words, of the church's mission for the redemption of the human race and its liberation from oppressive situation?" (*JW* §6) constitutive, and not just-integral and that word "constitutive" places action on behalf of social transformation with preaching and liturgical celebration (but also intrinsic to *their* correct understanding) as a necessary dimension of the church's mission.

This synodal document attempted successfully to begin the recovery of the biblical basis for social witness and to recover the

28

social dimension of key christian symbols notably God, Christ, faith and church. God is a God of justice 'the liberator of the oppressed and the defender of the poor'. Jesus reveals the indivisible relationship between 'love of God and love of neighbor' he preached the Father's special care for the needy and the oppressed. *Faith* is realized in love and service of the neighbor and in fulfillment of the demands of justice. The church's mission 'involves defending and promoting the dignity and fundamental rights of the human person'.

This recovery of the social and liberative dimension of key christian symbols (I listed only a few) is of course an on-going project of theologies of liberation and as it relates to oppressions other than those based on class analysis (poverty) it raises new issues and possibilities of the greatest interest and significance to the relationship between faith and culture.

Evangelii Nuntiandi

The third general assembly of the Synod of Bishops which met in 1974 dealt with evangelization but as they were unable to finalize an agreed-upon document the bishops left it to the pope to distill their findings. Thus Paul VI issued an apostolic exhortation on Evangelization in 1975.

We have already observed a shift from economics to politics in Paul VI's social teaching and we have seen his somewhat tentative shift from politics to culture. In *Evangelii Nuntiandi* (1975) that shift to *culture* is effected more forcefully. This is evident already in the statement issued by the synodal bishops which speaks of inculturating the Gospel among people of different cultures.

In the apostolic exhortation *Evangelii Nuntiandi* Paul VI related, evangelization to what he called the one absolute the Kingdom to which everything else is relative. The Magna Charta of the Kingdom is the Sermon on the Mount (Mt, 5-7). The rule or reign of God is meant to be one of "justice, mercy, love and truth": (Preface for Mass of Christ the King). Secondly, the pope gives prominence equally to witness and to preaching.

Paul VI also integrates the concept of *liberation* into his social theology and he describes it as being "from everything that

29

oppresses man ... above all from sin and the Evil One ..." The pope uses 'liberation' to discuss salvation but he refuses to identify the two. Nevertheless the project of liberation is established as a necessary aspect of the church's mission and at the same time the liberation which evangelization is concerned with is shown to be more integral than economic, social, political or cultural liberation in that it concerns the whole person who is to be regarded as open to 'the absolute even the divine Absolute'. (EN § 3,33)

Inculturation in EN

Evangelization is a complex process composed of many elements: "the renewal of humanity, witness, explicit proclamation, inner adherence, entry into the community, acceptance of signs, apostolic initiative" all of which belong together. (EN § 24)

Paul VI is less sanguine about culture than *Gaudium et Spes* was. In fact he says: "The split between the gospel and culture is without a doubt the drama of our time, just as it was of other times." Hence the explicit attention given to the "evangelization of culture and of cultures which is to be achieved not in a purely decorative way as it were by applying a thin veneer, but in a vital way, in depth and right to their very roots." The pope wishes to make the concrete human person the starting point in the context of relationship to others and to God. "The Gospel and evangelization ... are capable of permeating all (cultures) without becoming subject to any one of them." By evangelization of culture Paul VI means the evangelization of persons — their thought-patterns, their standards for making value-judgments, their interests, affectivity (what moves people) in brief the domain of meaning and vision where the deepest life-issues are concerned. (EN § 20) This, Paul VI says, is conversion and it should aim at people's consciences both personal and collective whence it seeks to eradicate sin. The implication seems to be that unjust structures in society, (e.g. slavery) can cause people to introject false opinions and attitudes ("I am a shifty, worthless person", "slavery is natural") and that change in thinking and attitudes can lead to structural social change. This may be possible but as one realizes the enormity of e.g. the arms race

30

today and its being interlinked with global supremacy, pursuit of scarce resources, and enormously lucrative contracts for corporations it cannot appear as an easy option to change such a system by changing attitudes.

At all events, without clearer indications of how social injustices linked to powerful interlocking militaristic, economic and political interests would be responsive to evangelization of culture one is suspicious that in *EN* Paul VI's option for a shift to the cultural represents less than what we would expect in view of the poverty, hunger, injustice and exploitation that people experience globally and within all nations.

John Paul II.

The extent of the present pope's social teaching is already enormous. Running through it both in the encyclicals and in discourses around the globe is the theme of "faith and culture". A subsidiary of that larger theme is the pope's teaching on "inculturation." In order to see the linkages between the formal social teaching and the culture thematic I propose to look at the pope's view of the human person, his anthropology, then his account of human rights, his understanding of culture and its evangelization. We shall then examine the pope's social teaching in light of his views on the gospel truly inculturated. Finally, we shall address critical questions to current practices by pope and curia which represent counter-trends to genuine inculturation and we shall revert to the pope's anthropology with a few critical questions.

Anthropology

For John Paul II the dignity of the human person is foundational in his social teaching.[8] This dignity is discernible by human reason since it is able to distinguish truth from falsehood, good from evil, and recognizes freedom as the fundamental condition of human existence. The pope identifies universal concern

---

[8] See: *Redemptor Hominis; Dives in Misericordia; Laborem Exercens, passim.*

for human rights as evidence of *the growing* recognition of human dignity by natural reason. At the level of faith human dignity is also grounded in each person's being created in the image of God. Further, following the Second Vatican Council the pope constantly reiterates that a) Christ is the key, the focal point and the goal of all human history, b) Christ reveals to human beings what it is to be human, c) Christ is personally united to each concrete man and woman, each individual person in their particularity. Thus, each human person is of value for her own sake and the personal dignity of each one represents the criterion by which all societies, cultures and institutions must be judged.

Human Rights

The dignity of concrete persons is recognized and secured only when they are in possession of the full array of human rights both those which pertain to material needs and those which fulfill spiritual needs. Each person has the right to life, food, work, clothing, housing, health-care, education, private and public religious expression, freedom of thought, to preserve and develop one's own ethnic, cultural and linguistic heritage, to be recognized and treated in keeping with the dignity of one's person in all circumstances.

If persons, concrete individuals, are denied any of their rights, either those which pertain to their material or spiritual side, then injustice is done, and the moral order is violated. If a society or nation systemically denies persons any of their rights then that society must be judged unjust according to the standard of human dignity which is properly recognized only when no rights are denied to any person.

Repeatedly, the pope refers to this understanding of the dignity of each person — a dignity, known by reason, reflecting God's image, secured by union with Christ — when he speaks about the church: "It is the mission of the church to travel the path of man because man — without any exception whatever — has been redeemed by Christ, and because with man — with each man, without any exception whatever, Christ is in a way united even

32

when he is unaware of it." [9] With special reference to the poor the pope argues that defending their dignity 'is not a luxury for the church' nor is it opportunism, it is the church's duty. Endorsing the 'preferential option for the poor' the Pope says "yes, the preference for the poor is a christian preference! It is a preference that expresses the concern of Christ, who came to proclaim a message of salvation to the poor, for the poor are indeed loved by God, and God it is who guarantees their rights." The church's mission of evangelization is towards all people but "she shows a special solidarity with those that are suffering and in need..." [10]

Culture

A constant theme in John Paul II's teaching is the necessity of evangelizing culture. While at some times the pope means by culture aesthetics, art and education more frequently he has a more complex concept of culture in mind, one which embraces the totality of a people's life-style including political and economic institutions and systems. With reference to this 'complex whole' the pope re-echoes Paul VI's view that evangelization of culture is a matter of the greatest urgency: "True culture is humanization, whereas non-culture and false cultures are dehumanizing. For this reason, in the choice of culture it is man's destiny that is at stake." By humanization the pope means "development (that) is carried out in all fields of reality in which man is situated and takes his place: in his spirituality and corporality, in the universe, in human and divine society. It is a question of a harmonious development, in which all the sectors to which the human being belongs are connected with one another." [11] Although it is not always expressed on each

---

[9] "The Eucharist is Love and Charity from which Brotherly Sharing Springs", Brazil: July 9, 1980. Text in *Brazil: Journey in the Light of the Eucharist*, St. Paul Edition, Boston 1980, p. 329 *Redemptor Hominis* § 14.

[10] "Justice and the Land" Bacolod, Philippines text in *Origins*, Vol. 10, No. 39, Feb. 12, 1981. p. 617. For an excellent, scholarly, nuanced account of the church and the poor in papal social thinking from Leo XIII to John Paul II see *Option for the Poor* by Donal Dorr, Orbis Books N.Y. 1983,

[11] "Gods Alliance with Man is the Work of Culture" Brazil: July 1, 1980, in *Brazil*, p. 71.

occasion the pope sees a dialectical relationship between cultural and other issues: "The problems of culture, science and education do not manifest themselves within nations and international relations independently and separately from other problems concerning human existence, such as the problem of peace or of hunger. Problems of culture are motivated (conditioned) by other dimensions of human existence, just as, in turn, they are conditioned as well."[12] Culture assumes this importance in the pope's thinking because he sees it as "the life of the spirit; it is the key which gives access to the deepest and most jealously guarded secrets of the life of peoples: it is the fundamental and unifying expression of their existence".[13]

Pope John Paul analyzes culture from its location in the deepest levels of the person to its national and global dimensions. All cultural advancement is rooted in thinking and loving; it springs from freedom and it requires a system free from all coercion in which to develop "culture which is born free, should also spread in a free system" and it should work to increase freedom.[14]

The pope frequently stresses the necessity for education so that people can participate in social life and enjoy their cultural heritage fully. He also stresses moral formation in the virtues of 'individual, social and religious life'. The pope often uses the expression "social love" to indicate that working for social justice and peace must be imbued with christian love, mercy and a spirit of reconciliation. Denying others their legitimate right to their culture by imposing one's own on them shows lack of social love.[15]

Evangelization of Culture

In order for a new synthesis between faith and culture to be achieved the church must evangelize culture. This consists in setting

---

[12] "The World as an Environment for Humanity" Popes address to UNESCO text in *Origins* Vol. 10, No. 4. June 12, 1980, pp. 58-64.

[13] "Every Diplomatic Community is a Testing Ground for Worldwide Concerns" Feb. 24, Tokyo. Text in *The Far East: Journey of Peace and Brotherhood*", St. Paul Editions, Boston: 1981, p. 270.

[14] "Gods Alliance with Man in the Work of Culture". Rio de Janeiro July 1, 1980 in *Brazil*, p. 72.

[15] *Ibid* p. 74. See *Redemptor Hominis* § 16.

the message and person of Jesus Christ before culture and announcing that in Christ and the Gospel the meaning of human existence is revealed. It is clear that the pope envisages here a task with two dimensions which complement each other: "One is the dimension of the evangelization of cultures, and the other is that of the defense of man and his cultural advancement". The pope continues: "The church must become all things to all peoples. There is a long and important process of inculturation ahead of us in order that the Gospel may penetrate the very soul of living cultures. By promoting this process, the church responds to people's deep aspirations and helps them come to the sphere of faith itself".[16]

Inculturation

One model which the pope has in mind for inculturation is the Incarnation itself. "The term 'acculturation' or 'inculturation' may be a neologism, but it expresses very well one factor of the great mystery of the incarnation! We can say of catechesis, as well as of evangelization in general, that it is called to bring the power of the Gospel into the very heart of culture and cultures." Just as the Incarnation testifies to the goodness of human nature so inculturation testifies to a goodness present in culture prior to evangelization and that goodness is "already a presence in germ of the divine Logos".[17]

In Africa in 1980 the pope encouraged the bishops to "carry on the task of inculturation of the Gospel for the good of each people, precisely so that Christ may be communicated to every man, woman and child. In this process, cultures themselves must be uplifted, transformed and permeated by Christ's original message of divine truth, without harming what is noble in them." But, he said this is a vast undertaking which "requires a great deal of theological lucidity, spiritual discernment, wisdom and prudence and also

---

[16] "The Dialogue between Faith and Culture" talk given by the pope at Sogang University, Seoul, S. Korea, May 5, 1985. Text in *Origins* Vol. 14, No. 2. May 24, 1984, p. 21.

[17] "Culture and Revelation" address to Biblical Scholars. Rome 1979. Text in *Origins* Vol. 9, No. 1. May 24, 1979, p. 15-16.

time". And he cites the example of Poland where the process of 'impregnating' the culture with christian values took centuries.[18]

Cyril & Methodius As Models

In July of 1985 in his encyclical "Slavorum Apostoli" the pope said that Cyril and Methodius had demonstrated an 'up-to-date' version of the catholicity of the church because of their recognition that the Gospel could be expressed in any language or culture. "The work of evangelization which they carried out — as pioneers in a territory inhabited by Slav peoples — contain both a model of what today is called 'inculturation' — the incarnation of the Gospel in native cultures — and also the introduction of these cultures into the life of the church. They are models also of love for the universal church and for the particular churches. "For full catholicity, every nation, every culture has its own part to play in the universal plan of salvation." [19]

The pope clearly sees that the Gospel, if inculturated in all societies, would provide a vital source of unity and communion in Europe and in the world. In August of 1985 and once again in Africa, the pope encouraged "a tireless effort at inculturation" so that the Gospel may penetrate all aspects of African life. The pope refers to this as a "second evangelization": "Now, African priests and laity, it is up to you to see that that grain (the Gospel) bears an original fruit, an authentically African one. To let the leaven cause the whole of the dough among you to rise: that is the whole point of the second evangelization, which is in your hands." [20]

Social Justice Implications

The role of the church, according to the pope, with reference to social justice, is to be critical and prophetic, that is, to denounce

---

[18] "Bring the Authentic Gospel to the African Cultures" Zaire May 3, 1980 text in *Africa: Apostolic Pilgrimage*, St. Paul Editions, Boston: 1980, p. 64.

[19] Encyclical *Slavorum Apostoli*. Text in *Origins*, Vol. 15, No. 8. July 18, 1985. See § 21, 22.

[20] "The Mystery of Renewal", Togo. Aug. 8, 1985. *Origins*, Vol. 15, No. 11, August 29, 1985, p. 167.

structural injustice, and ideologies which conceal the truth and render people unaware of their true situation; and to announce the possibility of a civilization of peace and love founded on justice.

It is, as Paul VI said, up to local communities or nations to do the requisite scientific, social analysis so that they can uncover the systemic causes of oppression within their own society or which they sustain or support in other societies or nations. The pope himself offers a systemic analysis of injustice — in outline — at several different levels.

Global Context

The global situation, the pope says in his first encyclical, represents as it were a "gigantic" development of the parable in the Bible of the rich banqueteer and the poor man Lazarus. Such are the disparities of income distribution and so great the gap between rich and poor that they "bring into question the financial, monetary, production and commercial mechanisms that, resting on various political pressures, support the world economy".[21] The world economy is wasteful and environmentally destructive, it is failing to meet peoples pressing needs and must be judged grossly inadequate because of the harm it does to countless concrete people.

In Canada in 1984 the pope spoke of the global situation in terms of exploitation of southern countries by northern ones: "...the South — becoming always poorer... and the North — becoming always richer. Richer too in the resources of weapons with which the superpowers and blocs can mutually threaten each other." Along with the threat of global annihilation there is the poverty issue: "...this poor South will judge the rich North. And the poor people and poor nations — poor in different ways, not only lacking food, but also deprived of freedom and other human rights — will judge those people who take these goods away from them, amassing to themselves the imperialistic monopoly of economic and political supremacy at the expense of others".[22]

---

[21] *Redemptor Hominis* § 16.

[22] "Development: The Progress of all the Disadvantaged" Homily, Edmonton, Alberta Canada text in *Origins*, Vol. 14, No. 16. Oct. 4, 1984, p. 247.

The pope tends to see one single oppressive economic system operating globally. He also sees totalitarian regimes which deny people their civil liberties, or perhaps more accurately, their freedom of conscience and spirit-related human rights.

It is clear that the pope's anthropology — the person in God's image, united to Christ with rights pertaining to the material and spiritual dimensions of life provides a criterion with which to judge both economic and political systems. Wherever any human rights are systematically denied persons, concrete flesh and blood persons, suffer indignities and injustice exists.

What has all this to do with his view of culture and its second evangelization which is called inculturation? This much in my opinion: Advanced industrial culture is thoroughly ideological and either for the economic reason of profit-maximization or for purposes of political control has evolved methods of controlling, bewitching and manipulating the masses. Persons are made into non-persons and they need to be awakened to their own plight and the plight of their societies national and global. A church which proclaims the gospel of the kingdom and which defends each person's dignity and full range of human rights can be powerful instrument of consciousness raising and a critical and prophetic force at local, national and global levels. Fidelity to Jesus Christ demands this of the church.

The church can only fulfill its prophetic and critical mission if, along with knowing the Gospel, it knows what is going on in social, economic, political and other systems. For this knowledge it needs autonomous human disciplines — collectively called culture — which also have truth about the human person. Dialectically complementing each other faith and culture can critique and correct whatever detracts from the dignity of human persons, any human person.

Critique

I believe this is a powerful message and I see in the shift to the cultural a necessary next step in the church's social teaching and ministry. So much for the positive part of the pope's message. What about his and contemporary curial practice? Here it seems to me that there is need also to be critical and prophetic.

First of all, the papal analysis which deals with armaments, hunger, poverty and ideologies, says little or nothing about patriarchy or the oppression of women who are not a cultural bloc or a local church but are half the human race and are oppressed — differently but really — in all cultures and, I might add, in all local churches as well as in the world church. Neither does the papal analysis say much about class, sexuality or racism as oppressions, despite their prevalence on the global scene.

Secondly, despite its internationalization the curia, particularly the Sacred Congregation for the Doctrine of the Faith, is bureaucratic and authoritarian and at times downright unjust — I refer especially to the treatment of Fr. Boff and the manner in which dissent on the issue of abortion and other sexual and theological issues is being dealt with at the present time. A church that preaches justice and human rights must be just and must respect the full range of all person's rights. Moreover, consider the irony involved in the fact that the synod that dealt most extensively with inculturation — that of 1974 — did not issue its own synodal statement. Instead, the pope issued an apostolic exhortation that distilled the thinking of the synod. But when one recalls the dissatisfaction that conservative circles felt concerning "Justice in the World" of 1971 and its use of the word "constitutive" to refer to the relationship between socialjustice work and the mission of the church one cannot but feel that there is a reluctance in Rome to allow the constitutional participation by the representatives of the College of Bishops — the Synod — and by national hierarchies in the real conduct of the government of the church even in their own spheres of competence. Examples can be multipled: the U.S. Hierarchy must petition three times to receive permission to administer communion in the hand; the Dutch Synod, the refusal to discuss the celibacy issue despite requests from national conferences of bishops to do so. In light of how centralized authority is exercised what hope is there for an inculturation that is more than superficial or cosmetic? [23]

There can be religious as well as economic or political imperialism. This brings me to my final point: There is something at

---

[23] See Paul Surlis "Laying Claim: The Synod Must Define Itself" *Commonweal*, Nov. 15, 1985, p. 629.

least apparently imperialistic about the claim to have the full truth about the human person and about the claim that Jesus Christ has united himself to every concrete person. The latter assertion, despite its apparent concreteness is abstractly formulated. Surely the pope would not hold that Jesus is united with the oppressor equally as with the victim! Also, one must ask how will this claim sound in the ears of persons of other faiths — but especially in Jewish ears since Jews have been persecuted in the name of Jesus throughout much of christian history.

Our world is pluralistic not only with reference to a world-church and local churches but with reference to other religions and their localizations. Even where local catholic churches are concerned they may be conservative, liberal or liberationist and they may live in cultures that are moribund or pathological. In other words 'inculturation' as an anthropological turn — and a necessary one — faces an empirical world of complex cultural variety and interaction and therefore in conjunction with theoretical frameworks tremendous amounts of field work need to be done in the best anthropological tradition. Just as European culture has undergone a certain relativization with reference to the recognition of other cultures so the church at Rome and its administrative structures must be prepared to be reformed and renewed as the input from other local churches continues to make itself felt across the face of the entire church.

Paul Surlis

Thomas Langan

ACCOMMODATING CULTURES WITHOUT DISSOLVING THE UNITY OF THE FAITH

A. The Challenge of "Inculturation"

Judging from the tenor of the discussions during F.I.U.C.'s seminar on "inculturation" at Tantur, Jerusalem, in September, 1985, the Church appears to be still in a "diastolic" phase, — the movement is still towards decentralization. If this movement were to become as extreme as the cramping "sistolic" phase which followed as reaction to the great missionary expansion and the fracturing of the Church in the Protestant revolt of the Sixteenth century, we may be in for some extremes of subjectivization, immanentization, and ultimately a tendency towards dissolution of the Catholic Church.

This would be ironic. At the very moment when a planetary culture is emerging, Catholics would take refuge in a nostalgic flight into local cultures, losing their nerve in the great struggle for the mind of mankind because, overly "liberal," they would be afraid of "imposing" the faith. Meantime, the one form of popular religion the Tantur group seemed united in detesting — the fundamentalist American sects — would go on successfully manipulating millions of immigrants and poor Latin Americans who are falling into their grips. Preoccupied with saving native cultures, these lovers of cultural diversity tend to ignore the real enemy of religion, and the greatest cultural force unleashed on the world today: technological, urban, secularist culture, which is uprooting millions in first, second and third world countries, and forming the professionals and "consumers" of a new kind of society, one that seems unprecedentedly immune to sound religious sentiment.

The Tantur seminar acknowledged intellectually that this vast new international society is indeed desperately in need of inculturation by the faith, but dialoguing with this massive culture was definitely not where their hearts were. I fear many in the Church are blocked by a kind of romanticism from putting their attention where it is most needed. The saving of traditional cultures is urgent and eminently worth while, as is securing social justice for the marginalized. But just as urgent is the Christian confrontation of the brave new world. Indeed, facing up to this most pressing modern challenge may well hold the key both to helping the poor and to preserving what can and ought to be preserved in traditional cultures.

Still, many helpful insights into the present situation and the challenge confronting our "world church" as it enters into communion with all the cultures emerged from these discussions. I would like first to state my understanding of these important "awarenesses" evident at Tantur and then go on to consider what I perceive to be certain limitations in our collective view, representative of thinking in many quarters of the Church today.

First, the modern approach to evangelization put forward by this group seems to me profoundly and sensitively Christian. It is motivated by the love which Jesus Christ Himself has for all peoples and for their hard — own accomplishments. At the same time, it shows a Christ — like special love for the poor and powerless. The desire to help the helpless pick themselves up from desperate situations has led Christian missionaries to devote their lives to the hardest work in the vineyard. From these experiences has grown the realization that the loving catechist needs to *listen* to the people, seeking to penetrate to the deepest sense of what their practices, their "sacramentals," and their conceptions mean. In this way, he can work with them so that everything positive in their culture may be illumined by the light of the faith and preserved in a sensitive synthesis with Christian experience.

Such listening presupposes an act of faith in the people one is evangelizing. The catechist has confidence that their religious experience contains treasures of insight deserving a permanent place in the House of the Lord. Instead of imposing a readymade, imported system of thought and life on an unsuspecting village, one seeks to bring the local symbols, profoundly understood, into communion with the universal symbols of the faith.

Second, there was enthusiasm for the idea that this process of mutual consciousness — raising between catechist and the people should be accompanied by efforts to help the people liberate themselves from elements in their situation which hamper them from the fullest possible realization of their dignity. This is seen as an essential part of building the Kingdom as Christ intends it. The

44

"sects," it seems, while working charitably with the people, do not seek to change unfortunate social structures. Rather, they tend to pacify the people, dulling their sense of injustice by "applying bandaids." So strong was the sense, in the Tantur meeting, of the need to join catechetics and work for social justice, I believe it important to pause here to reflect on some of the implications of this.

B. INCULTURATION AND "CONSCIENZIACION"

Some people interpret warnings from central Church authorities against direct political involvement as a lack of sympathy for the "marginalized" or as a lack of courage to speak out. Some see it as "Roman insensitivity" to the situation the poor are facing.

The problem, as I see it, lies in the danger that the individual missionary or catechist, in undertaking social consciousness raising, risks doing harm if he or she begins, perhaps without being aware of it, infiltrating *political ideology* into catechetical teaching. Some of the sinister forces lying behind the fabrication of ready — made ideologies can profit from this, with the catechist becoming unwitting agent of political forces with which, really, they have little sympathy. It is one thing to help a local group improve their material situation, and as part of this, to do something to shake fatalism or lethargy. Often the poor need to be made aware of ways to struggle against local oppression. But it is quite something else to indulge in mythologizing about "transnational corporations" (rarely named, never analyzed concretely!), "capitalist imperialism," or "Ronald Reagan's Star Wars" (without knowing much either about the intricacies of arms negotiations or the technology of intercontinental missile defense!) Spreading class hatred, feeding excessive nationalist passions, and encouraging resentment against those who are purportedly responsible for one's nation's plight is not Christian. Compassion is never an excuse for poor or manipulative "analyses" of vast situations one really knows very little about, nor for blaming other nations for anti-development attitudes stemming from the local culture. An eminent sociologist from the Hebrew University put it succinctly when we were discussing the situation that has arisen as the result of many church

45

people imbibing leftist ideology without realizing it: "Under the guise of raising social consciousness, some Catholic catechists are teaching hatred."

There is a certain arrogance (or is it just ignorance?) in the pretense of being able to analyze the vast and dynamic structures which provide the more distant framework of what is experienced locally as oppression. I am not suggesting that local social structures which permit coercion against poor peoples' efforts to organize cooperatives and to seek redress for despoilment of their land are anything but clear evils which any person of good faith will want to combat by every non-violent means at his disposal. Recognition of such immediately experienced, flagrant injustice need be mixed with no ideology, the "givens" of such a situation are quite understandable in themselves by the interested participant without his having to have recourse to pretentious explanations of how the struggles between "capitalism" and "socialism" impinge on the local situation.

One issue which inevitably comes up in certain situations if the missionary is going to participate in the people's struggle for justice is that of whether he is ever justified in advocating violence. What is the missionary to do when the local poor become convinced they must have recourse to armed rebellion to defend what little they possess? This is an issue in inculturation which was not discussed at Tantur. But I do not believe it should be side-stepped, if one is going to advocate serious involvement with the people. So, very hesitatingly, and for sake of discussion, I shall put forward an opinion.

I believe, first, he should use his good offices to try to get the elite to come to their senses. This is risky business, but the missionary, good Christ figure that he is, takes the burden of risk on himself. If he survives this intervention physically, and after exhausting all efforts at peaceful pressure, he may have no alternative but to stand aside as his people go to war. He should not, as an agent of the gospel, emulate Pope Julius II and lead the troops into battle. Rather he should work ceaselessly and at whatever risk to himself to bring about a just peace, exploiting every opportunity to get the leaders of both sides of the bloody conflict to compromise and stop the fighting, but seeking to make the elite realize that lasting peace can only come with justice, and that demands a significant improvement in the lot of the desperately poor. The missionary will then be a peacemaker, and an agent of justice, and his witness, his martyrdom, may be complete.

There are many who believe that catechesis should not be mixed up with social justice issues, and that it really has nothing essential to do with development. But I fail to see how anyone can come into an utterly depressed situation to bring the message of God's love and his command to master the earth and to prepare the way for the eternal kingdom without *instinctively* pitching in to help in any way he can to relieve the misery and suffering he encounters. Since the Jesuit "reductions" in Seventeenth century Paraguay and Brebeuf's concern for the lot of the Hurons, this has indeed been the instinctive reaction of most Christian missionaries. He may indeed be limited to "applying bandaids," he may not be able to do much about changing some of the profounder causes of the misery, but he does what he can. It does not help, indeed I believe it worsens a bad situation, to spread hatred and resentment, whether among his people or among his fellow intellectuals, through uttering wide-swinging ideological opinions about the national and international situation, essential aspects of which he very likely does not know. Without meaning to, he may contribute to an intellectual climate which actually helps the most repressive regimes in the world, or create an atmosphere unfavorable to approaches to production which can eventually furnish the capital surplus to invest in education, health care, housing and better transport for the mass of the people.

Above all else, one should guard against turning the liturgy into a political occasion. It is wrong, in my view, to abuse the captive audience at Mass with hints of political analysis, whether penetrating or half-baked — the perpetrator never knows, and always thinks his analysis is infallible! When this is done, however, well-meaningly, I believe it constitutes a serious abuse of clerical power, a dangerous new form of clericalism.

C. THE SCOPE FOR EXPERIMENT

How far should local churches be allowed to go in developing native liturgies into which have been absorbed many elements from indigenous religions?

The seminar was agreed that an understanding of the people's own traditional spirituality not only permits the missionary to commune with them *where they actually are*, but it yields riches for absorption into the ceaselessly growing universal treasurehouse of Christian symbol. So too use of indigenous traditional forms in the community's sacred celebrations eases access and enriches the liturgy at the same time. Dance, songs, particular postures, different kinds of offerings — with all these, there seems little problem.

But the core of the Mass should always and everywhere be maintained in universally recognizable form. The reasons for this seem to me obvious: 1. In the universal Church, it should be possible for a Catholic to go to Mass anywhere and find himself at home in His Fathers house, he should be recognizably among the People of God, clearly in the *Catholic Church*. 2. In its core, the Eucharistic sacrifice is unchanging, Christians are united across the centuries with the Last Supper. So whatever the enthusiasm expended on "inculturation," we want to remain clear that all the People of God are being brought to the same Table of the Lord. 3. The words approved for the ordo constitute a careful synthesis and balance of texts, stretching from King David's time, through the Age of the Prophets, the words of Christ Himself, from the early Church, the great hymns of the Middle ages, down to carefully reflected upon modern additions. They are magnificent texts, expressive of the common faith and experience of all Christians. Is there not a touch of arrogance in thinking that I can make up, often on the spot, better poetry? Add to them, outside the canon, to be sure, but with discretion and much thought. But leave the faithful the consolation, the sense of communion with an ancient and universal community.

Are there any exceptions where the Mass might, for instance, be virtually "osmosed" into Hindu forms of worship, and this for good reasons? The situation faced by Catholics in India, as described during the Tantur seminar by Father Ignatius Hirudayam, S.J., presents the challenge he describes so well as "achieving a successful summit meeting." In undertaking dialogue with persons coming from a great and ancient tradition possessing a rich "Scripture" and liturgy of its own, the partners in dialogue must approach eachother as equals. It is a quite different situation from what we might call the "teacher-pupil" relationship which

48

occurs when a well educated exponent of a rich intellectual heritage encounters a very simple person who is going to learn from him a set of new symbols for reflecting on an order of phenomena with which he has not been familiar.

What is necessary for a successful "summit meeting" is not an ascension but rather a descent to the foundations of the respective spiritual mountains, a descent of discovery down into the profoundest level of meaning possessed by the symbols and liturgical practices of both traditions. The goal, says father Ignatius, is above all discovery of new and deeper layers of meaning in one's own tradition, as well as the new respect and understanding which is gained for the tradition of the other.

But it is one thing to study the thought and liturgy of another tradition with utmost openness and sympathy, and quite something else to introduce the others' symbols into the Mass itself. Such a subsuming of, for instance, Hindu symbols into the Catholic Mass either demands successful translation and integration of the Hindu symbols into the meaning-structure of the Eucharistic sacrifice; or presupposes a complete equivalence of significance at some profound level.

Can either be? I do not see how anyone can judge who has not either participated in the experiment or at least studied with great care and discernment the tradition in question. For 18 years, in Father Ignatius' center in Madras careful reflection and experimentation has been going on. The liturgy which has resulted is beautiful and moving. The essentials of the Mass are retained and clearly recognizable. But from a mere film, no one would presume to judge what, long range, the effects of this will be, or even of its present appropriateness.

Such an important and obviously needed tentative raises with new urgency the question of how the Church can allow scope for such experimentation, while assuring that the Catholic Church continues to give the witness, demanded by Christ Himself, that we be one. The question of authority cannot be ignored. The role of the Pope and bishops, and their responsibility both to the needs of the local flock and to the demands of the universal Church is critical. But then neither can one ignore the need for communication, indispensable for the proper exercise of authority.

D. Prerequisite for the Good Exercise of Authority: Communication

In the epoch of the "world church" the oldest and vastest institution on earth is faced with the need to improve communications rapidly. Neither its hierarchical-clerical structure nor the predominance of a Thomistic concept of truth, devoid of a sense of historicity, have equipped the institution well for the task of listening and for shepherding with suppleness and with loving concern of the Other's otherness.

Consider all the challenges to listen:

Local — bishops must hear all estates within their flocks, — the poor, the middle class, the rich, priests, religious, young people, family heads, the old. And all estates must learn to listen to the voice of the bishop. (The letters of our Cardinal Archbishop in Toronto are not infrequently thrown in the wastebasket!) In an anti-authoritarian age, this requires new humility and a sense of obedience that is, for the present, largely lacking.

National — The bishops must listen to spokesmen from all parts of the country, not just the rich center, and the bishops must listen to eachother. (The polarization within some bishops' conferences is scandalous). And the whole nation, Catholic and noncatholic alike, should hear the bishops when, having listened with discernment to the whole nation, they speak on problems illumined by the light of the Gospel.

Regional — Nations must listen to their neighbors with whom they almost always stand in some political tension — strong must hear weak, the weak must listen to the voices of compassion and concern coming from among the strong, and they must learn to understand that those who hold the levers of power are in fact faced with many and complex problems.

Planetary — Rome must put itself into a position where it virtually forces itself to have to listen to spokesmen for all God's people, a vast undertaking of consultation. Rome has the responsibility of bringing the experience of one part and different classes to bear on

50

other parts and other classes within the Church. No other institution is so well situated to be an instrument of communication. In building the People of God as Christ wants it, this role of planetary communication facilitator is literally God-given.

Once one surpasses the most local level, the institutional structures are so large they are easy prey for manipulation by persons so convinced they possess *the* truth, they have no need to listen to anyone else. It is easy to give the appearance of favoring "participation," and then never really listen. It is useful to sketch a "worse case scenario" of how this might be done.

One establishes a small committee of officials not too well informed about the complex issues. This committee is served by a small, dedicated group of functionaries, all of the same ideological bent. Announcing "participation," the committee holds hearings, being careful to do so with small groups, keeping ideologically different persons apart. With as many groups as possible talking at cross purposes, the poor officials find that the advice cancels out. And they are overwhelmed. The functionaries, with a quite free hand, then draft the document, attempting to counter some of the good arguments advanced against their underlying ideological position, and ignoring the even better ones they cannot answer. This draft is then presented by the committee to a very large body of responsible officials. It is too long and complex for meaningful alteration. If the draft is then made public, one accepts submissions from critics. The same drafting group of functionaries then recasts the final draft to respond to some of these criticisms, but without altering the basic position they intended to advance all along. The final version is then issued as the official view of the large body, and is ready to be taught in all the schools.

In case any reader may think this worse case scenario unlikely to happen in an era in which the Church stresses the need for openness and communication, I would point out that the small group of functionaries responsible for drafting the U. S. bishops' pastoral letter on nuclear arms and their letter on the U. S. economy (some of the key people were the same on both drafting groups) contained *not one single person* with any sympathy for the political position of the present U. S. administration, recently re-elected by a record majority. Had the persons who so tightly control this process

51

agreed to admit into the inner sanctum just *one* intelligent "sinner against the light" they would at least have been aided in developing better arguments on behalf of their position. (I would be willing to bet that the small group of righteous ideologues giving this wonderful witness to the Church's ability to listen consider themselves very open to foreign cultures, ideal people for carrying out the sensitive tasks of inculturation!)

What is the way around the kind of ideologues who think only they are interested in peace and only they have any real compassion for the poor, in other words, what is the path to real listening on the part of those responsible for large structures? Without some way of responding to the real problems of pluralistic society, the Church will find it difficult to keep proper control over the complex processes of "inculturation" and societal critique which are actually going on.

Vatican II called for lay involvement, and clearly spelled out the political and economic realm as the proper field of the laity. I believe the key may lie partly in a new model for lay involvement.

A proposal has been made in North America to constitute for the bishops a kind of "think tank" regulated by a constitution designed to assure that it would be drawn from men and women in all the principal walks of life — workers, engineers, mothers, doctors, small business men, higher managers, etc. From their midsts would come the drafting committees as needed, with particular experts being added ad hoc. The group as a whole would first discuss the issues the bishops propose to address, both to get a feel for them and to identify in their midst the persons best able to take on the particular drafting exercise. The resulting draft would pass through two or more small committees of bishops, small, so as to allow real debate and criticism, and two or three to provide variety of view. Finally, the document would have to be passed by the plenary of the bishops' council.

The whole design is meant to avoid both ideological dogmatism of the kind currently depressing many well-informed and caring North American Catholics, disappointed by the fruits of what is set out as a "participatory" process of preparing pastoral letters, but which they see producing seriously flawed results.

Some such structure may prove useful at all levels where participation is really called for. Inculturation of the faith into secular, urban, high technology society requires dialogue with those who enjoy an intimate acquaintance with its complex problems. These are to be found principally among the laity. With a broad group of experienced people to call on, the hierarchy will be able to avoid the narrowness of the manipulating professionals. Given the nature of our society, this is imperative.

Thomas Langan

Rodger Van Allen

CATHOLICISM IN THE UNITED STATES:
SOME ELEMENTS OF CREATIVE INCULTURATION

Introduction

This paper will ultimately maintain and defend the proposition that Catholicism within the United States is somewhat creatively inculturated, that is, that it is attempting to seize upon and build on the positive features of the culture while questioning, challenging and confronting the more dubious features of the culture. We will begin, however, by reviewing and outlining the major successive phases in the developing history of Catholics in this country. We will then turn to the key themes encountered in this experience and the contemporary application of these themes which leads to our positive appraisal in the phrase "creatively inculturated."

Phases in the Developing History of Catholics in the United States

I find four major phases in the developing history of Catholics in the U. S. as charted from the time of this new nation's 1776 Declaration of Independence from Great Britain. Catholics have gone (1) from aristocratic origins, (2) through immigrant Catholic coming of age, (3) to maturity and identity crisis, and (4) to creative inculturation.[1]

I use the phrase "from aristocratic origins" to characterize the period from 1776 to 1815, the death of the first Catholic bishop, John Carroll. Catholics were less than one percent of the new nation's four million inhabitants in 1776.[2] Jesuits had been among

---

[1] See similar language used in Rodger Van Allen, *The Commonweal and American Catholicism* (Philadelphia: Fortress Press, 1974).

[2] John Cogley, *Catholic America* (New York: Doubleday, 1974), p. 7. In the historical overview in this paper I also rely on James Hennesey's excellent *American Catholics: A History of the Roman Catholic Community in the United States* (New York: Oxford University Press, 1981).

the 1634 colonists of Maryland and Catholics belonged to the political and social elite of that colony. In 1734, Jesuits founded St. Joseph's in Philadelphia, the first urban Catholic church in the thirteen colonies, but even in its physical appearance and location, the church was discreetly hidden away as Catholics typically took a low profile in a U.S. that was dominantly Protestant and wary, suspicious, and frequently hostile to Catholics. The aristocratic tone of Catholic presence in this period was set by the Carroll family and a small group of other Catholic families in Maryland and Virginia whose wealth and dedication to the new nation made them accepted and respected members of the leadership elite. No one, it seems, risked a greater personal fortune than Charles Carroll when he signed the Declaration of Independence. It was his cousin, John, who was named Superior of the Mission in the thirteen United States in 1784. In 1788, a petition on behalf of priests in the United States asked that "at least in this first instance" [3] choice of a bishop be left to them and when the request was granted, John Carroll was chosen by a vote of 24 to 2.

Bishop Carroll has been aptly described as "the right man, in the right place, at the right time." [4] He was wholehearted in both his Catholic and American identity and he saw no incompatibility between the two. Though firmly rooted in an understanding of the needs of a predominantly poor Catholic population, Carroll moved easily among the elite too. For example, it is perhaps a sign of the respect he commanded that when Carroll visited in Boston, Governor John Hancock insisted that he stay in the Governor's mansion. [5] With the aristocratic tone given by Carroll's leadership, a small and relatively inconspicuous Catholic presence moved toward a quiet assimilation. In 1813, President Kirkland of Harvard was ready to "admit the possible, nay more, the presumptive Christianity of a virtuous and devout Roman Catholic." [6]

---

[3] Thomas O'Brien Hanley, *The John Carroll Papers* (3 vols.: Notre Dame University Press, 1976) 1:279-82; see Hennesey, *op. cit.*, p. 87.

[4] Cogley, *op. cit.*, p. 27.

[5] Don Brophy and Edythe Westenhaver, eds., *The Story of Catholics in America* (New York: Paulist Press, 1978), 22.

[6] As quoted in Hennesey, *op. cit.*, p. 117.

I've called the second phase in the developing history of Catholics in the United States, "through immigrant Catholic coming of age." This long phase begins not long after Bishop Carroll's death in 1815 and continues essentially until 1960. The major change is in the number of Catholics who go from an almost negligible presence in our first phase to a situation where fully one in every four persons is Roman Catholic and Catholicism is the largest single religious denomination. This change was the result of major waves of immigration. The Irish led this floodtide of immigration and came so swiftly through the 1840's that already by 1850, Catholics were the largest single body of churchgoers in the nation.[7] Germans, Poles, Italians, Slovaks and others followed in a continuous stream that was only stopped by more restrictive immigration policies in the 1920's. Economic necessity was the biggest reason for leaving the "old country" to come to America. Most immigrants were poor and uneducated and they met class prejudice from some Americans, and economic prejudice from others at the influx of so much cheap labor. These factors compounded the anti-Catholic prejudice that grew in virulence and became persistent throughout this period. The occasional anti-Catholic violence that marked the nineteenth century was essentially gone by the first decades of the twentieth century but anti-Catholicism continued in ways that were somewhat more subtle but no less powerful. Catholic immigrants themselves, however, were strong in their identification as Americans. Their lives generally were better and more hopeful in the United States than they would have been had they not emigrated, and this was a comfort, despite the hostility they sometimes experienced. They were dedicated to the principles of the United States even though the treatment they received from some Americans at times betrayed those principles. As James Hennesey states, "The Catholic community became, if anything, superpatriotic."[8]

The papal condemnation of "Americanism" occurred during this period, in 1899. Pope Leo XIII was careful not to make any specific charge against the church in the United States, its bishops or any identifiable groups or individuals. Historian Thomas McAvoy

---

[7] *Ibid.*, p. 126.
[8] *Ibid.*

referred to Americanism correctly as a "phantom heresy." [9] At issue, however, was the model of inculturation of the Catholic church in the U. S. and especially the extent to which that model might be imitated in France. In 1895, Leo XIII had praised the church's growth and the situation in which Catholicism was "unopposed by the Constitution and government ... fettered by no hostile legislation, protected ... by the common laws ... free to live and act without hindrance." But he also warned others not to imitate the American style of separation of church and state and even expressed his view that the church in the U. S. "would bring forth more abundant fruit if, in addition to liberty, she enjoyed the favor of the laws and patronage of public authority." [10] A dismayed Bishop John Ireland wrote privately that "the unfortunate allusion to Church and State cannot be explained to Americans." [11]

The rather adolescent exercise of the United States' emerging military muscle against Spain in 1898 is now commonly regarded by historians as crudely imperialistic, but almost all the U. S. bishops publicly supported the war in florid "patriotic" language. One leading Americanist prelate called it a contest between "all that is old and vile and mean and rotten and cruel and false in Europe" and all that is "free and noble and open and true and humane in America." [12] Such simpleminded and erroneous notions probably contributed to the condemnation of Americanism.

The major consequence of the condemnation of Americanism was that the leadership of Catholicism in the U. S. lost their confidence, and the optimistic, experimental and venturesome Catholicism of the late nineteenth century gave way to a conservative, cautious, hesitant Catholicism, that thought pastoral competence in meeting the needs of Catholics in the U. S. could be

---

[9] Thomas T. McAvoy, *The Great Crisis in American Catholic History* (Chicago: Henry Regnery Co., 1957).

[10] In John Tracy Ellis, ed., *Documents of American Catholic History* (Milwaukee: Bruce, 1962), "Pope Leo XIII's Encyclical *Longinqua Oceani* (January 6, 1985), pp. 495-507, at p. 498.

[11] As quoted in John Tracy Ellis, *The Life of James Cardinal Gibbons* (2 vols.; Milwaukee: Bruce, 1952) 2:30; see Hennesey, *op. cit.*, p. 200.

[12] Denis J. O'Connell as quoted in Gerald P. Fogarty, *The Vatican and the Americanist Crisis: Denis J. O'Connell, American Agent in Rome, 1895-1903* (Rome: Università Gregoriana Editrice, 1974), p. 280.

found simply in an increasingly legalistic application of Roman directives. In addition, as John Cogley states: "For many years, with the memory of the "phantom heresy" in mind, Catholic scholars were hesitant to speculate seriously about the theological significance of the American experience, lest they too should run the risk of being charged with heresy." [13]

Ordinary Catholics, as distinguished from intellectuals, were little aware of the Americanism affair. The "immigrant Catholic coming of age" phase continued as uprooted Catholics from around the world landed in America and drove themselves harder and faster than almost any other groups [14] as they struggled for a decent and tidy life and still better opportunities for the next generation. It was the savy of the streets that led them to instruct their children: "Get a good education. It's the one thing no one can ever take away from you." The continuing hostility toward Catholics seemed to reinforce rather than threaten Catholic identity. Concerns for Catholic identity and a good education gave powerful impetus to the continued expansion of Catholic education.

Martin Marty has described the restrictive immigration laws of 1920 and 1924 as one of the few things Protestant Americans could .agree on at that time.[15] Within the carefully orchestrated quota systems built into the laws was a religious and racist bias especially against the overwhelmingly Catholic Southern and Eastern European immigrants who had predominated in the throngs of newcomers in the first two decades of the 1900's. Even highly placed intellectual leaders such as Francis Walker, the president of MIT, could write of their nervousness at the corruption of the gene pool in the U. S. by the influx of these "inferior" human specimens.[16] So a combination of prejudices played a big part in cutting the flow of immigrants.

Catholics worked very hard at showing that they really were good Americans who had no desire either to subvert or dominate

    [13] Cogley, *op. cit.*, pp. 63-64.
    [14] See Andrew M. Greeley, *The American Catholic: A Social Portrait* (New York: Basic Books, 1976).
    [15] Martin E. Marty, *Righteous Empire: The Protestant Experience in America* (New York: The Dial Press, 1970), p. 211.
    [16] As quoted in Andrew M. Greeley, *An Ugly Little Secret: Anti-Catholicism in North America* (Kansas City: Sheed, Andrews and McMeel, Inc., 1977), p. 18.

the U.S. politically. There has never been a Catholic political party in the United States. Catholics, especially the Irish, had been numerous and prominent in the two major political parties, the Republicans and the Democrats, especially the latter, since it was considered the party of the labor movement and Catholics were essentially of the laboring class. In 1928, Governor Alfred E. Smith of New York, a Catholic, was named the presidential candidate of his party. Smith was thoroughly committed to the principle of separation of church and state and had never even remotely considered any other arrangement. Confronted by quotations from papal encyclicals holding this separation to be tolerable rather than ideal, Smith responded, quite honestly, that he had never even heard of these teachings though he had been a devout Catholic from childhood.[17] Despite his unambiguous statements of support for religious liberty, Smith was soundly defeated by Herbert Hoover. The electoral vote was 444-87. Whether it was Smith's religion that defeated him is controverted. It is not controverted that there was a great deal of anti-Catholic feeling expressed during the campaign.

Stung by the expressions of bigotry many Catholics felt reconfirmed in their withdrawal from many aspects of American life. They celebrated the individual achievements of certain Catholic athletes and entertainers, and took a special symbolic pleasure in Notre Dame football victories, but they remained in a social and cultural detachment that has been called the "Catholic ghetto."[18] Within this ghetto and within the Catholic consciousness, however, there was no sense of inferiority, nor any diminution of either a Catholic or American identity, but the period was still one of an immigrant Catholicism *coming* of age rather than an immigrant Catholicism *come* of age. As late as 1959, as perceptive an observer as John Cogley worried that Catholics were in but not of the country, acting always "as if its problems were not our problems, as if its failures were not our own, as if the challenges confronting it were not confronting us."[19]

---

[17] Hennesey, *op. cit.*, p. 252.

[18] Cogley, *op. cit.*, pp. 135-54.

[19] John Cogley, "The Catholic and the Liberal Society," *America* (July 4, 1959), p. 495 as quoted by David J. O'Brien in Irene Woodward, ed., *The Catholic Church: The United States Experience* (New York: Paulist Press, 1979), p. 5. The Woodward book is an excellent collection of essays on inculturation.

The key event in the transition from an immigrant Catholic coming of age period to what we have called the "maturity and identity crisis" phase was the candidacy and the election of John F. Kennedy as the first Catholic president of the United States. Anti-Catholicism was by no means absent from the campaign, but Kennedy's personal style and charm, conveyed to the public now by television, and Kennedy's calm and clear responses to sincere questions of Protestants and others, combined to produce a narrow victory for the young senator from Massachusetts.

The Kennedy presidency symbolized and to some degree effected change for Catholics in the United States.[20] It was the identity of the U.S. itself that changed, however, and the change affected many citizens, not just Catholics. The President is the presider. Symbolism is important. Before Kennedy, the symbols were those of a country Protestant in identity, presided over by Protestant presidents. For many, the thought of a Catholic in the White House seemed as inappropriate as would perhaps the thought of a Moslem President of Notre Dame University seem to many Catholics. After Kennedy, the symbolism changed and with this came broad changes for Catholics. Catholics went from a suspect and second class status in the society to a full and matured partnership. The change, aided by the attractiveness and freshness of Pope John XXIII, happened so swiftly and so decisively that younger Catholics today are baffled by any description of the hostile dimensions of pre-Kennedy Catholicism.

The early 1960's were years of great enthusiasm for the *aggiornamento* Catholicism of Vatican II, for public service, the Peace Corps, and identification with American ideals, and a matured and come of age Catholicism participated in all of this in more than full measure. Rapid progress was made in establishing real civil rights for black Americans, thanks again to the new power of television and the remarkable leadership of the Reverend Martin Luther King, Jr.. Catholic Americans in their new phase of matured citizenship had "made it" politically and had progressed remarkably in economic and social life too.[21] They were no longer under their old burden of showing with bursts of super-patriotism that they

---

[20] See Van Allen, *op. cit.*, pp. 127-40.
[21] See Greeley, *op. cit.*

really were good Americans. As the Vietnam War progressed into the late '60's, many Catholics realized that being a good Catholic and a good American meant that one had a responsibility to speak out and take action when one's country was proceeding wrongly. This was not easy, however, Catholics, and many other Americans too, were quite conscious of the generous and honorable role of the United States in World War II, and of the personal decency and goodness of the young Americans drafted for military service in combat in Vietnam. To have to say that a big mistake in policy was being made was traumatic. It challenged the identity of a great number of Americans whether they were Catholic Americans or not.

A similarly traumatic event developed specifically for Catholics, in 1968, with the issuance of the encyclical *Humanae Vitae*, repeating the absolute prohibition of contraception. Many Catholics, some as early as the economically hard pressed 1930's, had concluded to the practical necessity for some genuinely reliable means for birth regulation. For many these genuinely reliable means included some form of contraception officially condemned by the papal letter. The reaffirmation of the official condemnation contradicted the experience of marriage for these Catholics and led them to conclude that their church as well as their government was clearly capable of making big mistakes. They had long known that neither their government nor their church was perfect but they were not prepared for the scope of the blunders they felt that Vietnam and *Humanae Vitae* represented.[22] The effect of these twin traumas was alienating and contributed heavily to the identity crisis aspect of this "maturity and identity crisis" phase of the experience of Catholics in the United States.

It is difficult to put a date on the emergence of our fourth phase, that which we have described as the creative inculturation phase. The mere use of the phrase can sound triumphalistic. Surely the concrete reality in any of these periods is some combination of good and bad, creative and uncreative. Surely there is subjectivity to the value judgments one must make in even using such language. Our task at this conference, however, as I see it, is not to withdraw to some narrowly defensive piece of unassailable territory, but to

---

[22] *Ibid.*

64

risk the venturesome and contemporary assessments that are the stuff out of which can come practical insight and action.

This "creative inculturation" phase is one in which a matured Catholicism within the U.S. is authentically attempting to seize upon and build on the positive features and values within the culture while questioning, challenging and confronting the more dubitous and wrong features and values of the culture.

We have already seen action of this sort in the increasingly critical and ultimately condemnatory action taken by Catholicism in the U.S. against the Vietnam War. The 1971 statement of the U.S. Catholic bishops applying the tests of the just-war doctrine to that conflict and concluding that it failed the test of proportionality, i.e., was clearly producing more evil than good,[23] is the only time in history that the church in any nation has practically and conclusively applied the just-war doctrine to render a negative judgment on a conflict waged by their own nation.

In 1973, another event brought critical action when the U.S. Supreme Court gave sweeping approval to abortion. The bishops spoke out clearly saying the court's opinion "is wrong and is entirely contrary to the fundamental principles of morality."[24] Catholic laity in great measure agreed, and many Catholics felt a reaffirmation of their more distinctive identity[25] in resisting the rush toward a more or less routine acceptance of abortion.

In the 1980's two substantial episcopal statements gave further articulation to this creative inculturation of Catholicism in the U.S. The first, "The Challenge of Peace: God's Promise and Our Response"[26] was a pastoral letter on war and peace, formed through a lengthy process of consultation and revision, that uniquely captured media and popular attention with the searching realism and hope with which it addressed the problems of nuclear arms. The letter stated itself to be "more an invitation to continue the new appraisal of war and peace than a final synthesis of the results of such appraisal," but such sincere humility seemed to

---

[23] See *Quest for Justice* (Washington: U.S. Catholic Conference, 1978), a collection of statements by the U.S. bishops.

[24] *Ibid.*, p. 154.

[25] See Brophy and Westenhaver, *op. cit.*, p. 148.

[26] Washington: U.S. Catholic Conference, 1983.

increase respect for the statement rather than undercut it in any way. Americans liked the idea that the statement didn't presume to say the last word on the subject, but still had the courage and competence to make a genuinely helpful contribution toward sanity in the nuclear age. In 1985, a first draft of a pastoral letter on "Catholic Social Teaching and the U.S. Economy" [27] demonstrates the willingness of the church in the U.S. to evaluate economic structures from the perspective of "the dignity of the human person realized in community with others." This too is evidence of the creative inculturation of Catholicism.

We have thus far described our four major periods in the evolution of Catholicism in the U.S. We have seen it go (1) from aristocratic origins, (2) through immigrant Catholic coming of age, (3) to maturity and identity crisis, and (4) to creative inculturation. We turn now to consider some of the key elements and features in this experience.

The Voluntary Church

Freedom, the freedom to associate with the church or not associate with the church, has been fundamental to the experience of Catholics in the United States. This "voluntaryism" or voluntary principle is basic to the understanding of religion in general in American society. This principle emerged as part of a pragmatic realism in dealing with the fact of pluralism. The beginnings of this pragmatic realism can be found among those pluralistic settlers of Maryland in 1634 who knew that they had enough other problems to deal with and had thus better learn to live together religiously. Voluntaryism and the separation of church and state, however, did not begin in America. Indeed, the *Acts of the Apostles* tells us that the early Christian community rejected the notion of a state religion and appealed instead to the need "to obey God rather than man," what we would call the rights of conscience and free choice. Speaking of the voluntaryism of the primitive church, James Luther Adams points out that the Christian viewed the church in its origin

---

[27] The first draft is published in Origins, Vol. 14, Nos. 22/23 (November 15, 1984), pp. 337-83.

66

and development as the work of divine grace, yet, "on the human side the church was a voluntary association." [28]

> The church appealed to the individual for a voluntary decision to join the movement. It rejected civic religion, the rule of Caesar and of territoriality in the sphere of religious commitment and faith; it transcended the ethnic bonds of traditional Judaism; it gave to the individual certain responsibilities in the new organization; it was open to people of all classes and races; it gave new status to the common man, to the slave, and to women; and it soon developed forms of responsibility with respect to charity and philanthropy....[29]

A remarkable expansion of members and changed historical circumstances brought the early church into the era of Christendom with its unified structure of society in a church-state. One can find vestigial remnants of this era in the lingering taxes for church support in a few countries even today. Generally, however, the modern era of the voluntary church began with the demand of the sects for the separation of church and state. Adams states that "although the struggle for voluntaryism on a large scale in the church began over two hundred and fifty years ago, it was not achieved generally and officially in the United States until the nineteenth century—that is, apart from the colonies that from the beginning had had no establishment." [30]

In our recap of the history of Catholics in the United States we have seen that they were consistent in their· desire for this voluntaryism and sought nothing more than their right to be a free church in a free society. Rome could not always understand the wisdom of this American experience. Recall, for example, Pope Leo XIII's 1895 admonition, which we noted earlier, that the church in the U.S. "would bring forth more abundant fruit if, in addition to liberty, she enjoyed the favor of the laws and the patronage of public authority." [31]

---

[28] James Luther Adams, "The Voluntary Principle in the Forming of American Religion," in Elwyn A. Smith, ed., *The Religion of the Republic* (Philadelphia: Fortress Press, 1971), p. 221.

[29] *Ibid.*

[30] *Ibid.*, p. 223.

[31] See footnote § 10.

Richard McBrien in his essay, "The American Contribution to Ecclesiology," argues that "there is a distinctively American contribution to the notion of church in the sense that our being Catholic in the United States makes a difference to the kind of Catholic Christianity we embody." [32] The American understanding of the nature and mission of the church, McBrien states, arises from the American experience with the principle of voluntaryism, the separation of church and state, and political democracy.

A Democratic Style

McBrien points out that resistance to the democratization of the Catholic church is often based on the assumption that democracy is equivalent simply to majoritarianism. With this understanding, the truth of Catholic doctrine would be determined largely by a show of hands. But by "political democracy," McBrien does not mean rule by the majority but rather "consent to, and participation in, the decision-making, governing process by all whom that process affects." [33]

John A. Coleman holds that at the Second Vatican Council, there emerged a new church-society model which holds promise for the needs of the American church. Coleman calls this Vatican II model a "cultural-pastoral or voluntary association model." [34] In it the church sees itself "as a voluntary association within a wider non-Catholic or not explicitly Catholic host society whose autonomous competencies the church respects." Coleman maintains that the Council provided the theological underpinning for "a host of American values as these are captured in the conciliar code-word, collegiality." He speaks of democracy, pluralism, tolerance, civil and religious liberties, the rightful autonomy of the secular, the voluntary principle of organizations and participant co-responsibility for the direction of organizations and accountability by management.

---

[32] In Woodward, op. cit., pp. 73-89, at p. 74. For McBrien "distinctively" does not mean uniquely or exclusively, but characteristically or descriptively.

[33] *Ibid.*, p. 75.

[34] In Woodward, *op. cit.*, pp. 43-67, at p. 57. The essay is titled "American Catholicism and Social Theology."

Coleman concludes that the voluntary church, when successful, is clearly superior to culture Christianity and established religion in engaging genuine commitments of its members.[35]

The analysis of Avery Dulles on the American experience of church is not essentially different from that of John Coleman and Richard McBrien, but the tone is more cautious and conservative. Dulles warns that the American experience of church "should not be simplistically patterned on the American political experience."[36] Dulles says that those who are convinced that the American political tradition of freedom, democracy, and reformability provides adequate norms for the church "will in time encounter serious difficulties in being a committed Catholic." Like McBrien, he points out that "Catholic Christianity cannot be governed from below by majority votes." He does see Vatican II as acknowledging that values such as personal freedom, equality, and fraternity have "a certain applicability in the Church, "but he finds the strong sacramental and hierarchical structures of the church effective in opposing the modern threat of radical individualism. He praises the Council for breaking the stranglehold of modern "traditionalism" by recovering a more ancient and dynamic idea of tradition.[37]

Catholics in the U.S. have no desire to dictate doctrine through majoritarian democracy, they value the sacramental and hierarchical dimensions of their church, and they do not want a church that offers them no distinction from secular society. They do, however, want a church that is genuinely participatory and fair. They do want a democratic style in church life. This has been manifested most clearly in extensive studies in the U.S. of what Catholics are looking for from their local church, their parish. Four things are mentioned consistently: good preaching; lots of programs, activities, and services; worthwhile counselling with problem situations; and a *democratic style of church leadership*.[38] As

---

[35] *Ibid.*, p. 60.

[36] Avery Dulles, "Vatican II and the American Experience of Church," in Gerald M. Fagin, ed., *Vatican II: Open Questions and New Horizons* (Wilmington, DE: Michael Glazier, Inc., 1984), pp. 38-58, at p. 55.

[37] *Ibid.*, pp. 56-57.

[38] See Andrew M. Greeley, *Crisis in the Church* (Chicago: Thomas More, 1979); also Philip Murnion, *The Parish Project Reader* (Washington).

Richard McBrien states: "Just as Jesus was not dispensed from the routine dynamics of the physiological and biological organism that was his human nature, so the church is not dispensed from the dynamics of human communities." Its decision-making processes, says McBrien, "must involve some measure of *conspiratio* (literally: a breathing together)." In saying this, McBrien feels that he is expressing the participatoriness that is at the core of the American experience. He also finds this American experience consonant with the most basic principles of Catholic ecclesiology: (1) that the church is the people of God before it is a hierarchically-structured institution; and (2) that it is a collegial community, not a monarchial society.[39] I find McBrien to be correct both in his ecclesiological summary and his discernment of the core of the American experience. I also find it impressive that there is evidence that this democratic style of leadership seems to be more effective pastorally. The Parish Project of the National Conference of Catholic Bishops studied 329 parishes that enjoyed a reputation for vitality. In a time of declining Mass attendance these parishes typically experienced no such loss and in fact generally had an increase. The priest who led this study project, Philip Murnion comments:

> These parishes evidence what might be called a democratic style of leadership in a number of ways. First, they are somewhat more likely than others to use the variety of ministers and ministries available: laity, religious, and deacons as staff members and parishioners as eucharistic ministers, lectors, and leaders of various programs. Second, to further encourage parishioner leadership, half of these parishes have had some kind of ministry training. Third, the staff meets regularly, more than half every week and 80 percent at least every two or three weeks. Fourth, 92 percent of these parishes have parish councils in operation or in formation. When asked to identify the quality that most accounts for vitality in their parishes, these parishes most frequently identified the variety of opportunities they provide for people to participate.[40]

---

[39] In Woodward, *op. cit.*, pp. 85-87.
[40] Philip Murnion, "The Local Church," *The Living Light* Vol. 19, No. 4 (Winter, 1982), p. 302.

70

A Healthy and Practical Realism

In addition to its vigorous life in an atmosphere of voluntaryism, and its fondness for a democratic style, I am also struck by another aspect of the creative inculturation of Catholicism in the United States that I would call its healthy and practical realism. To make this point more concretely, I will give three illustrations. The first will focus on the "Challenge of Peace" pastoral; the second, on the important speech of Archbishop John Quinn at the 1980 Synod of Bishops; and the third, the "Chicago Declaration of Christian Concern" issued by a largely lay group of Catholics in December 1977.

The Challenge of Peace pastoral letter had the courage to undertake an extensive analysis and teaching on the toughest moral problem of our era, the arms race and nuclear weapons. It was, however, the healthy and practical realism that was part of the American experience of church that did not permit the ducking of this issue. It also was the basis for the extensive consultation (a democratic style) that was such an important part of the genesis of this document. It was also the basis for the humility with which this document was presented. The bishops did not presume to have said the last word on the topic. They worked seriously with these issues, and while some have differed with aspects of their concrete application of principles, the bishops opted not only to risk this but to welcome it if it would contribute in a practical way.[41]

The second illustration of this healthy and practical realism concerns the speech which was given in the name of the National Conference of Catholic Bishops of the United States by Archbishop John R. Quinn at the 1980 Synod of Bishops. He began by affirming his personal acceptance of the teaching of *Humanae Vitae*, but he also noted the widespread and practical disagreement with its absolute prohibition of contraception. He pointed out that this opposition was found even among those "whose dedication to the Church is beyond doubt." Quoting Pope Paul VI's remark that *Humanae Vitae* was "not a complete treatment regarding man in

---

[41] See Jim Castelli, *The Bishops and the Bomb: Waging Peace in a Nuclear Age* (New York: Doubleday, 1984) for a splendid account of the steps in the development of the document.

this sphere of marriage" and that this was an immense field to which the magisterium of the Church "could and perhaps should return with a fuller and more organic and synthetic exposition," Quinn made a concrete proposal for dealing with "the harmful impasse."[42] He called for the Holy See to initiate a formal dialogue with Catholic theologians that would begin with "a listening phase" that would include both theologians who support the teaching on contraception and those who do not, bearing in mind Pope Leo XIII's principle that "the Church has nothing to fear from the truth." The second phase would be comprised of an effort to work toward the resolution of this problematic situation.

Quinn's proposal is admirably direct and simple. In light of the structure of the Synod it might even be dismissed by some as naive. Consider the following comment on the structure of the Synod[43]:

> The lay auditors were not representative of the Church but were in fact firm supporters and promoters of natural family planning. The majority of Catholic families which practice birth control were not represented. Nor were dissenting theologians welcome at the Synod. As a result no true dialogue was really possible. Any criticism of *Humanae Vitae* was considered scandalous. ... Some bishops were afraid to say what they really thought because they would be misrepresented by the press or seen as challenging Popes Paul VI and John Paul II. Bishop after bishop stood and quoted the Pope to himself, which is a strange exercise for a body that is supposed to advise the Pope. After all, does he not know what he has said?

It cannot be determined whether the American Catholic bishops really knew beforehand just how resistant the atmosphere and structure of the Synod would be. Some might even dismiss their stance, as it was expressed in Quinn's speech, as some kind of

---

[42] "'New Context' for Contraception Teaching," *Origins*, Vol. 10, No. 17 (Oct. 9, 1980), pp. 263-67. See also Jan Grootaers and Joseph A. Selling, The 1980 Synod of Bishops "On the Role of the Family,": *An Exposition of the Event and an Analysis of Its Texts* (Leuven: Leuven University Press, 1983) which suggests that there are basic structural defects in the Synod.

[43] Thomas J. Reese, "The Close of the Synod," *America*, Vol. 143, No. 14 (Nov. 8, 1980), p. 281.

survival of American innocence.[44] I find their stance, however, not foolish, but wise, and expressive of that practical realism and wisdom that knows the pastoral harm that may follow the manipulation or should we say subversion of the Synod process?

My third illustration of this healthy and practical realism in Catholicism in the United States concerns a document called the Chicago Declaration.[45]

> Issued in mid-December 1977, the Declaration charged that a wholesome and significant movement in the Church — the involvement of lay people in many church ministries — has led to a devaluation of the unique ministry of lay men and women. The tendency has been to see lay ministry and involvement in some church related activity, i.e., religious education, pastoral care for the sick and elderly, or readers in church on Sunday. Thus lay ministry is seen as the laity's participation in work traditionally assigned to priests or sisters.

The signers feel that the welcome involvement of lay people in many church ministries has in fact upstaged, distracted and confused many laity into thinking that *this* was what religion was all about. Where, they ask, is that compelling vision of lay Christians in society? The laity, who spend most of their time and energy in the professional and occupational world "appear to have been deserted," while many in the Church exhaust their energies on internal issues "albeit important ones, such as the ordination of women and a married clergy." In its final sentence, the Declaration comments: "It would be one of the great ironies of history if the era of Vatican II which opened the windows of the Church to the world were to close with a Church turned in upon herself."[46]

---

[44] I've appropriated the phrase from William M. Halsey, *The Survival of American Innocence: Catholicism in an Era of Disillusionment (1920-1940)*, (Notre Dame: University of Notre Dame, 1980).

[45] See Russell Barta, ed., *Challenge to the Laity* (Huntington, IN: *Our Sunday Visitor*, 1980), which contains the Declaration and the papers presented at a 1979 conference on it at Notre Dame University.

[46] *Ibid.*, pp. 25-26.

I have elsewhere[47] commented extensively on the Declaration, here I will simply comment that it reflects that healthy and practical realism within Catholicism in the U.S. that recognizes that the church is for the world and not vice-versa. The call of the Gospel is to reach out creatively in society. Indeed, it is a call to be actively and creatively inculturated.

Conclusion

In this paper, we have traced Catholicism in the United States from its small aristocratic origins, through its massive immigrant Catholic coming of age phase, to its maturity and identity crisis period and into its creative inculturation. The distinctive elements we have identified in this process are voluntaryism, a democratic style, and a healthy and practical realism. We have seen Catholicism come of age in such a way as to see it recognize its responsibility to humbly and yet courageously raise questions on structures and issues in the society and in the church.

Arij Roest Crollius has distinguished what he calls "three moments in the process of inculturation."[48] In the first stage, *translation*, the Church makes its first contact with a new culture, but presents the Christian message and life in the forms of another culture. I believe that in this paper, in choosing to ignore the French and Spanish influence in North America, and in focussing instead on Archbishop John Carroll and a continuous line of development since then, we have in fact entered at Crollius' stage two, *assimilation*. Carroll's stamp on the church was that of an assimilated native clergyman, although actual numbers of Catholics were quite small. Further, even the characteristics of voluntaryism, a democratic style,

---

[47] In Robert J. Daly, ed., *Rising from History: American Catholic Theology Looks to the Future* (College Theology Society Annual Publication, Volume 30), Lanham, Maryland: College Theology Society - University Press of America Co-Publication, 1986.

[48] Arij Roest Crolliu's, Theoneste Nkeramihigo, *What Is So New About Inculturation?* (Rome: Pontifical Gregorian University, 1984), p. 14. This volume is number five in the series, *Inculturation: Working Papers on Living Faith and Cultures*, edited by Arij A. Roest Crollius, published by Centre "Cultures and Religions" — Pontifical Gregorian University.

74

and a healthy and practical realism, can be seen continuously from the time of Carroll. In the analysis of Roest Crollius of stage two, assimilation, the young church ";may sometimes tend to adapt itself more passively to the surrounding culture."[49] This was basically true in the American experience. I find the so-called Americanizers, Archbishop John Ireland, Bishop John Keane, and others, to have been fundamentally correct in their positive appraisal of the opportunities for the church in the American context, with its official religious neutrality. They were not, however, sufficiently detached from the culture to serve it with a creatively critical perspective.[50] In my view, however, Roest Crollius' stage three, *transformation*, has emerged in the American experience. Thus, the church does have a more active role in the transformation of this culture. This is achieved, however, within an essentially communitarian notion of church that operates in accord with the voluntaryism that we have noted. This communitarian notion of church does not, however, dismiss the need for episcopal leadership and courage, but it does define the context in which it is exercised.

I fully concur with the Roest Crollius notion of inculturation as "a process of growth toward maturity"[51] and I feel that the American experience offers one model of this. I have focussed for the most part on the positive historical circumstances of the church in the United States, but I do not deny that one could easily note a catalogue of negative elements such as individualism, conspicuous consumption, militarism, racism, etc.[52] I don't think, however, that an excessive focus on these themes, such as Cardinal Ratzinger seems to have brought forward with denunciatory rhetoric, is helpful or creative.[53] Frankly, I am also tired of hearing and seeing appraisals of Catholicism in Poland and Eastern Europe that find

---

[49] *Ibid.*

[50] See, for example, Dorothy Dohen, *Nationalism and American Catholicism* (New York: Sheed and Ward, 1967).

[51] *Op. cit.*, p. 15.

[52] See McBrien, *op. cit.*

[53] Elini Dimmler, "Ratzinger Criticizes Marxism, Hedonism, Bishops Conferences," *Religious News Service* release, November 28, 1984, pp. 7-8, based on a three-day interview with the Italian Catholic magazine *Jesus*.

everything to be perfect ("the only zone where Catholicism is not in crisis" says Ratzinger). This is contrasted with a view of Catholicism in the U. S. that sees it as the examplar of crisis. On the contrary, I find a Catholicism that is creatively inculturated, lived by a vigorous Christian community in answer to a divine initiative, out of a participation in the life of Christ, and in the communion of the universal church.[54]

Rodger Van Allen

---

[54] See Roest Crollius, *op. cit.*, p. 15.

TIPOGRAFIA POLIGLOTTA DELLA PONTIFICIA UNIVERSITÀ GREGORIANA
PIAZZA DELLA PILOTTA, 4 - ROMA